WRITING
TELEVISION
COMEDY

WRITING
TELEVISION
COMEDY

Jerry Rannow

ALLWORTH PRESS
NEW YORK

04   03   02   01   00   5   4   3   2

Published by Allworth Press
An imprint of Allworth Communications
10 East 23rd Street, New York, NY 10010

Cover design by Douglas Design Associates, New York, NY

Page composition/typography by SR Desktop Services, Ridge, NY

Library of Congress Catalog-in-Publication Data:

Rannow, Jerry.
    Writing television comedy / by Jerry Rannow.
        p. cm.
    Includes index.
    ISBN 1-58115-042-3 (pbk.)
1. Television authorship. 2. Television comedies. I. Title

  PN 1992.7.R33 2000
808.2'25–dc21

                                                        99-059329

Printed in Canada

CONTENTS

- -

RIGHTS

My sincere appreciation to the following for permission to reproduce the material indicated:

Also a grateful nod to: Laura Sharp (Warner Bros.), Susan Edelist (Dreamworks), Jake Easton/Joshua Baur (20th Century-Fox), Johnnie Luevanos (Universal), Marcia Green (WGAw).

ACKNOWLEDGMENTS

I'd like to thank the following people who provided aid or influence in the creation of this book:

Jonathan Winters, Red Skelton, Steve Allen, Toby Rowe, John Fritz, Percy and Edna Helton, Frank Faylen, Jed and Toby Allan, Ruth Burch, George Kelly, Joe Endes, Sydney Pollack, John Travolta, Fred Urbanski, Jessie Wadsworth, E.J. Andre, Ricky Barr, Jewel Jaffe Ross, Martin Ross, Lawrence Carra, Ella Gerber, Ron Pallilo, Joe Gramm, John Schallert, Marilyn Budgen, Robert Hegyes, Jim Parker, Arnold Margolin, Angela Slater, William D'Angelo, Jon Kubichan, Lawrence Hilton Jacobs, John Sylvester White, Marcia Strassman, Debralee Scott, Eddie Applegate, Hank Jones, Jim and Judy Begg, Bernadette Lynch, Candy Howerton, Greg Strangis, Sam Strangis, Alan Sacks, James Komack, Michael Thoma, Chet Collier, Gabe Kaplan, Ray Arsenault, Audrey Hoobin, Rick Ray, Gary Cosay, Harry Bloom, Rich Eustis, Michael Elias, Harv Thompson,

Marshall Cook, Chris DeSmet, Jerry Apps, Howard Hesseman, Gaby and Susan Wilson, Eric Cohen, John Furia, Jamie Kijowski, Nicole Potter, Tad Crawford.

And a SPECIAL THANKS:

To the members of my family who have always supported my dreams—especially to Mom, for allowing me to be my quirky little self.

BIG INTRO

I believe that this is the first book ever written on TV comedy by someone who has actually written TV comedy. Sure, you'll see all kinds of books on the subject. One by a college professor whose only Hollywood experience was Mr. Toad's Wild Ride at Disneyland. Another by some expert who once shared story credit with six other people on an episode of *Barney* without the *Miller*. Don't listen to those people; listen to me. I've been there. I've spent over twenty-five years working in network television as a writer, producer, story editor, script consultant, actor, and whipping boy, so I'm intimate with the territory. Not only can I show you the ropes, but I can also teach you the difference between a slippery half-hitch and a square knot. I didn't attend all those Boy Scout meetings for nothing, y'know.

My years as a television writer and my schooling in hard knocks definitely qualify me as a top-notch instructor. I'll use a common-sense approach free from labels and academic definitions. I will not only teach you what to do and how to do it, but what not to do and how not to do it while still remaining on the studio payroll, which is a common practice among those in TVland.

I am about to share loads of practical experience, nonpractical experience, and some remarkably unorthodox perceptions about writing sitcom. I will give you an "insider's" look behind the scenes of the shows I have contributed to, some of them classics, never mind about the rest. I will use several script illustrations from actual teleplays—some of them current, others not so current, but well-remembered. I will provide you with a first-hand perspective of the sitcom world with play-by-play descriptions of what it's like to work with network and studio executives, agents, producers, directors, writers, and stars. I won't always use their real names; some of these people aren't dead yet, so unfortunately we'll have to wait.

What you are about to read will be instructive and, above all, entertaining. You will learn a great deal about the fun and the craft of writing scripts for laughs. I may get technical at times; if you don't like it, tough luck. Nobody ever said writing was easy. Except this one writer I knew, Howard Leek, who said writing WAS easy, which is why you've never heard of Howard Leek.

The not-so-simple fact is that writing is damned hard work and there's a lot of sweat, skill, and technique involved. This being the case, I will show you all the tricks and tools of the trade and how those tricky little tools can be used to your best advantage. One thing is guaranteed, I will never be dull. Dull teachers make for dull students, and I believe in having fun. My high school record of forced visits to the principal will vouch for this.

Writers like you are important to the future of television comedy. The TV industry is desperately in need of talented, courageous individuals who won't take no for an answer. Poop-disturbing writers who will stick up for themselves and not be afraid to tell show business executives that they have no guts, no brains, and should seriously consider going into retail sales at Sears.

You have talent. You know that or you never would have gotten out of the store without paying for this book. So sit back, relax, and get ready for an "E" ticket ride through the quirky, jerky, I-wouldn't-trade-it-for-a-minute world of SITCOM.

—JERRY RANNOW

I NEVER METAMORPHOSIS I DIDN'T LIKE

I was brought up in what could have been a pretty humorless atmosphere. I had lost two fathers by the time I was eleven and, as the oldest of five boys, I assumed a fatherhood role that consisted of trying to keep my four younger brothers entertained. Being silly, acting stupid, doing schtick—my brothers loved it. I got laughs and made everybody feel good; I was hooked on humor.

I actually remember radio. Listening to George Burns and Gracie Allen, Jack Benny, Edgar Bergen and Charlie McCarthy, and other comedy greats made me laugh. My ears were glued to the radio, never missing a chance for the writers to tickle my funnybone.

These radio scribes wrote some of the finest comedy ever written. Genuine wit. Copies are available, so take a listen. One episode of Don Ameche and Frances Langford in *The Bickersons* is better than a whole season of just about any comedy show currently on TV. It's not just the funny lines, but because we participate, visualize the scenes, the faces, the expressions in our own way. Radio is all ears. It's our play. The unique theatre of our minds.

These snippets of radio scripts from *The Bickersons,* created and written by Philip Rapp, will give you an excellent idea of what I am talking about:

John: What do you want me to do, Blanche? Should I call Doctor Hershey?

Blanche: No.

John: Well, what do you want? Are you really sick or is this just something you're doing to keep me awake, is that it?

Blanche: Maybe it is. It's the only way I can get any attention from you.

John: Attention? No husband in the world is more attentive than I am. Don't I always offer you half the newspaper at breakfast?

Blanche: You shouldn't read at the table at all—and when you drive the car up in front of the house, you might be a gentleman and help me in.

John: Help you in . . . ?

Blanche: Oh, no, I have to fling open the door and throw myself into the seat.

John: Well, I slow down, don't I?

*   *   *

Blanche: . . . Why didn't you let me have a big ceremony, John?

John: I wasn't working at the time. I didn't have any money.

Blanche: Well, you're working now and I want a real wedding with a big ceremony.

John: (gives up) Okay, I'll arrange it in the morning.

Blanche: You say it, but you won't do it. Do it now!

John: What??

Blanche: Go on—get up and let's get married.

John: Are you out of your mind, Blanche? It's almost four o'clock in the morning.

Blanche: (near tears) Why don't you say you're sorry you married me . . .

John: Because I'm not sorry.

Blanche: You don't act like you love me.

John: I act.

Blanche: Well, kiss me goodnight.

John: I'll kiss you goodnight in the morning.

Blanche: But why can't you kiss me now?

John: I'm not facing that way.

* * *

Blanche: (whimpers) Eight anniversaries and this is the most miserable of all!

John: It's no worse than last year . . .

Blanche: . . . Where's my anniversary present, John?

John: Oh, you won't like it.

Blanche: I know I won't, but I'd like to see it. I hope you didn't spend a lot of money.

John: I didn't spend a lot of money.

Blanche: Why not?

John: Because I didn't have a lot of money. Just a little old beach bathrobe. It cost eight dollars.

Blanche: Eight dollars?? Married eight years and you spend only eight dollars?

John: Now, listen Blanche . . .

Blanche: A dollar a year for washing your shirts, cooking your meals, darning your socks, raising your children . . .

John: We don't have any children.

Blanche: Well, what do you want for a dollar a year?!

* * *

Blanche: I bought a mink coat.

John: A mink coat?? How much was it?

Blanche: Lie down, John.

John: Blanche, how dare you go out and spend money on a mink coat? We can't afford a mink coat!

Blanche: Now don't scream at me . . .

John: I deny myself everything. I've been tearing down the old curtains, wearing them for suspenders—I sew collars on my underwear to save on shirts—I never spend a penny on myself and she has to have a mink coat!

Blanche: You had your shoes shined last Saturday.
John: I haven't GOT any shoes—I had my feet painted black!

Philip Rapp: Now, there's a writer who could make people laugh.

SEEDS OF SILLINESS

My family came late to the TV age. We were not the first or even the tenth on our block to have a television set, so I spent many a night outside the downtown appliance store window watching Milton Berle bring his zany brand of burlesque comedy to the newly-discovered medium.

We finally got a TV—a used Philco with one of those round screens—and my life began to take on new meaning. It was my *Dream On* period and, although I thought Howdy Doody was a spastic in need of drug therapy, I was suddenly exposed to a world of talents I had never experienced before. People who came from radio to TV— Ernie Kovacs, Steve Allen, Sid Caesar, Imogene Coca, and all of their writers.

These huge talents left me with the infectious feeling that maybe comedy wasn't such a bad way to make a living, so I would copy them, take from the best, and my high school skits were hits. I rationalized my "borrowing" with the idea that I was forwarding comedy culture to the masses. Eventually, this lie got to me and I was forced to write some original jokes and a lot of them scored! Now I was cookin'! There's nothing like the rush you get hearing laughs for a line you didn't steal.

TO BE OR WHAT TO BE

Actually, I never intended to be a writer. All through high school and college I was preparing myself for a career as a professional actor. Master Thespian! At the time, the notion of becoming a writer just never occurred to me. I took little note of the fact that I wrote those skits for the variety shows or that I had my own column in the school newspapers or that I ghost-wrote love letters for my friends with great success, and now they're all divorced and blame me.

My goal to be a great actor led me to New York City where I studied acting with a well-known teacher you've never heard of. I attended numerous auditions where somebody else got the part, and I channeled this constant rejection by spraying the cockroaches who roomed with me. I used a can of hair spray left by the former tenant. It made the roaches hair look so good they doubled their population.

This was not my idea of a career. I could no longer live like this. This was not my dream. In my dream, Ann-Margret was ripping my clothes off, but enough about my dream. My dream has changed. It's Uma Thurman now, and I don't want to talk about it. Writers are private people, y'know.

In my quest to fulfill my dream, I scraped together all the money I had and visited exotic Hollywood for a week. In that one week, I landed an agent, a one-line acting job on *My Three Sons,* and I immediately made up my mind that Hollywood was the place to be. I broke the lease on my New York apartment, moved all my belongings to an L.A. apartment with tanned cockroaches, and didn't work again for the next two years.

Was I discouraged? You bet I was. I was living on Spam and used bubble gum. How could I put myself through this? How long could I go on beating myself up? It was surprisingly easy. I had a dream.

A WINTER'S FANTASY

Around the time I was about to start barbecuing my jockey shorts, something pretty terrific happened. I snagged a "regular" acting job on *The Jonathan Winters Show.* Out of five hundred auditioners, they chose me! Suddenly, I was fully employed as an actor on a CBS variety show where, every week, I would be doing sketch comedy with Jonathan Winters himself.

This acting job would turn out to be the beginning of my career as a PROFESSIONAL WRITER.

The Jonathan Winters Show was a golden time in my life. I couldn't wait to get to rehearsals every day. Working with Winters was like a trip around the world on acid. One day, Winters was "Ragnar," the Viking King; the next day he was "Beano," the meanest six-year-old on the block. Working one on one with Winters every day left me no choice but to play along, to improvise back—to be Ragnar's son and Beano's buddy—to grow as a creative person. Working with

Jonathan Winters was like going to "comedy college," and I was head-ed for a master's in thinking on my feet.

The only negative that comes to mind is a doozy: The scripts were LOUSY. A roomful of highly paid writers were turning out pret-ty unfunny stuff for a very funny man. At first, I doubted my own hunches about this. I assumed that professional TV writers turned in good work. Not so. There was as much crap being written then as there is now. So, if you see something on one of today's TV shows that you don't think is particularly funny, stick to that opinion because you're right.

Oh, sure, the audiences were laughing, but they were amused by the ad-libbed antics of Winters himself and not his anemic material. This is when I decided that I could be a writer. "I CAN DO BETTER THAN THIS," I told myself, and I set to work writing the definitive Jonathan Winters sketch. It was a great sketch—a hilarious sketch—and as soon as I finished it, the show was canceled and my sketch shipped out to chortle heaven.

Was I discouraged? You bet I was. Was I a quitter? Never! I had committed the ultimate crime. I had written with intent to sell, and this sentenced me to a life at the keyboard.

OILING THE BREAK

I wrote every day—a lot of stuff that nobody wanted to see until I met the producer of a show called *Love, American Style* at a party. In a huge move toward furthering my career, I got up the nerve to ask if he would read a "spec" script I had written for his show. ("Spec" stands for speculative, which in television means "Be willing to work for nothing or you'll never make a cent.") The producer had apparently overdosed on the guacamole because he graciously said he would be happy to read my spec script. Oh, joy and rapture, what luck!

There was a catch, of course. As convincingly dynamic as I had been, I now had to sit down and actually WRITE a spec script for his show. (Isn't it funny how people always say they "sit down" to write? This is not always the case. I know writers who write standing up, lying down, and a few who won't get out of bed at all.)

Anyhow, I immediately got on the phone and called every-body I knew who was in or closely allied to the TV business. I needed script samples. I had no idea of what a sitcom script looked like. I vowed that I wasn't going to be ranked as an amateur, and luck was with me. I tracked down several scripts, studied the format, and now that I knew what a professional script looked like, I began to teach myself to write sitcom.

I completed my script, submitted it to the producer, and he liked it so much he immediately offered me a staff position as STORY EDITOR. How about that! This writing racket was a snap. My first television script and I was a working writer! I was on staff! I had an office, a secretary; the weenies and beans in the Paramount commissary were mine for only $3.95, including cornbread!

I had ARRIVED, and I lived for the moment when someone would ask me what I did for a living and I could proudly boast, "I am a WRITER!"

A week later, the producer was fired, and I was back to roaming parties in search of another break. Was I discouraged? No, just impossible to be around. Was I a quitter? Never! I had invested ten bucks in a used typewriter, and I wasn't about to blow that kind of dough.

I got my hands on many books similar to, but not nearly as good as, this one, and they started to lead me on the right path. I began in earnest to absorb and learn the craft of writing. I was an actor settling comfortably into my new "role" as a professional writer.

I was no longer torn between acting and writing. I had come to the realization that writing was a more convenient way to spend idle hours than acting. Writing is a solitary endeavor, whereas acting requires the participation of others. It was like a choice of masturbation over group therapy. I had no choice but to write every day.

A year later, the highly perceptive producer who liked my script was miraculously hired back, and my writing career officially began!

I'll never forget my first day at the studio as I drove through the famous "Paramount Gate" in triumph! All eyes were on ME—mainly because no one had actually driven through the Paramount Gate in thirty years.

I whipped my car into my very own parking spot, and when I saw that my name had been quickly stenciled over the name of some poor writer who had just been canned, I knew I had arrived. I was part of an exclusive club of showbiz professionals—the kind who were actually working. A few weeks later, the Writers' Guild of America—the union of which I had proudly become a member—went on strike, and I was out of work again.

Was I discouraged? DON'T ASK! Was I a quitter? NEVER! I had a dream, and I was determined to pursue that dream into a reality. Never lose your dream. Water it every day. When you achieve one dream, always have another one ready. Channel your dreams onto paper. Set aside a time each day to write. Write and keep on writing. Pile up those pages.

Writing is a discipline requiring you to keep putting your ideas down on paper. Papers joined into scripts pave the way to that sought-after break. Writing takes practice and practice prepares you to perform when opportunity dances it's way into your life. People need to laugh. That's what writers like us are here for.

JUMP-STARTING THE FUNNYBONE

Humor is necessary to life. Chuckles and hoo-ha's provide us with a solid grasp on our sanity. Humor helps us communicate because it says a mouthful in a flash, and gets people to listen. A humorous person is regarded as someone worth paying attention to whether that person has anything to say or not.

Everyone is born with a sense of humor. The capacity for humorous expression has a home within all of us, it just needs to be whipped out and paraded around once in a while. We all have a "funnybone," a flair for the ridiculous that needs to be cultivated. Whether we acknowledge that flair in our bone is up to us.

You're a lot funnier than you think you are. Everyone (except for an IRS auditor) is capable of saying or thinking funny things on a daily basis. You just have to learn to trust it in yourself.

I don't think you'd be reading this book if you didn't think you could be funny. All I want to do is stimulate your mind and increase your awareness, so you can immediately identify and have fun with the humor in life. I'm not saying that I can just teach anyone to be funny, but I can help you discover and enhance that funnybone that is lurking somewhere inside you.

Return to those thrilling days of yesteryear, when you were just a sprout and you amused your Uncle Chet and your Aunt Doris by simply saying whatever burst into your little head. Your Dad or Mom would proudly point at you and say: "Oh, our little cutie is so funny!" Then, later, when you stopped being cute and turned into a teenager, you'd say something equally clever and your Dad or Mom would point at you and growl: "Don't you be funny with me!"

So, as you can plainly see, our level of humorous expression has a great deal to do with our upbringing. If you were raised in a family with humor, lucky you. If your parents were brain-dead dweebs whose idea of fun was to shoot the neighbor's dog in the leg, don't worry about it because "funny" isn't necessarily hereditary. So, what the hey—take a chance—shake off those years of adult repression that have blocked that natural spontaneity. I want you to—

DARE TO SOUND STUPID!

That's right—trust that little voice within you that knows when something is funny. Now, plop down on that whoopee cushion and go on to the next paragraph.

SPEAK UP, KID!

As a young, yet cool, teenaged dude, observing the absurdities of life, I was shy and afraid to risk conveying my thoughts aloud to anyone. At parties, I would tend to mumble my quips to myself and someone with X-ray hearing would always ask: "Jerry, what did you say?" All heads would swivel in my direction. "What did Jerry say?" I was stuck like a nose under a tractor wheel. Now, I'd have to repeat something I inwardly thought was very funny to a room full of critics who were waiting to be entertained, so I would re-enact my humorous gem. One snicker, a few groans, loads of blank stares. The original moment was not to be recaptured. You had to be there. If I'd had the nerve at the time, I would have boldly delivered my line on the spot, for all to hear, and to hell with the consequences.

Today, I have achieved nerve. I say what I think is funny whenever and wherever I wish. I have found a direction in life skillfully guided by nerve and blind stupidity. Even if people don't think what I say is funny, the people I say it to are still (in the backs of their minds) trying to think of something to say in return because it's basic human nature to want to TOP the other person. My challenge has awakened a seed of humor within these people, and they will never go back to being as boring as they used to be. At least I certainly hope not.

THE RICHARD SIMMONS SCHOOL FOR WRITERS

As a sitcom veteran, the question I am most often asked is: "Why did you wear THAT?" The second most-asked question is: "How can you just sit down and write?" Well, the fact is, most writers can't. Starting to write is a terrifying concept, and it demands a certain amount of foreplay. If that means what I think you think it means—hey, whatever gets you there. The point is, you can't write comedy unless you exercise your mind, and you should never exercise without warming up.

Here are a few, quick HUMOR EXERCISES that I use with my writing students. You'll find these very useful for shifting your brain into comedy mode:

- Play "show and tell" with yourself. Pick up some inanimate object, stand in front of a mirror and tell yourself about this object. What do you find funny about it? Get as silly as you can get. As Will Shakespeare once said, "Silliness is the heart of comedy."
- Did anything really stupid happen to you or someone you know? An embarrassing or awkward situation? Write it down. Then go back and EXAGGERATE it. Then exaggerate the exaggeration; tell a whopper.
- What kinds of things tick you off—really make you nuts? Write them down. Then EMBELLISH them. Devise comically fiendish ways to get rid of these bothersome things— zap your mind into space.
- Ask yourself bizarre QUESTIONS that are open to equally bizarre ANSWERS. For example, if I said, "Do you mind if

I take your picture in the nude?" what would you say? Don't cling to reality; stretch your mind. DARE TO SOUND STUPID!

- Put your own silly CAPTIONS on photos. (You'll usually find these photos in magazines and newspapers.) You can also cut the captions off single-panel CARTOONS and provide your own joke lines. This can become seriously addictive, but who cares? It's a jim-dandy way to f-l-e-x your comedy think muscle.
- Create a JOKE—your very own bon mot, a wry, humorous, off-the-wall observation of human events or behavior. Watch a comedian you enjoy for inspiration.
- Write a short, autobiographical PARAGRAPH making "fun" of yourself. If you can't poke fun at yourself, you'll never be free to poke fun at the world around you.

Give these exercises a shot. I think you'll find this kind of foreplay very useful, and it could possibly lead to a hot date with success.

As comedy warm-ups go, my personal favorite is the grocery list. I sit down, pencil poised over paper, and begin to create my grocery list. The first draft is pretty straightforward stuff: "milk, bread, eggs . . ." By draft three or four, I'm really starting to wail, adding stuff like "abnormal brain, eye of newt, and pom fronzbees"—a product that does not exist, but sounds silly and tickles me to no end. And, guess what—I'm WRITING!

THE IDEA

Well, friend, the time has come for me to grasp your little hand in mine and lead you on a journey through the creative process—a necessary trip for any writer who wants to write a "spec" script for that much-maligned form we call SITCOM.

Now, the word Sitcom is short for Situation Comedy, which translates into a comedy based on situations.

A good sitcom story IDEA places the star (or supporting character) into a situation in need of a resolution, which will cause the character to respond in unexpected, exaggerated, and hugely side-splitting ways.

The comedy TELEPLAY is the bastard of the literary family. It's basic purpose is to tell an engaging story, supported by boffo laughs, followed by an enormous check.

A teleplay isn't like a screenplay or a playplay, it's a recent historic invention containing twenty-four minutes of wit and wisdom interrupted by commercials, which are often wittier and wiser than the show.

A teleplay begins with a seed. That seed is an IDEA. People are always asking me where I get my ideas. When I glare at them in silence for a few minutes they usually go away. It's none of their business where I get my ideas!

I am, however, altering this policy for you, the reader of this book. I figure that, since this chapter is on ideas, I'd better talk about where I get my ideas or this chapter is already over, which is not such a good idea.

I get my ideas from LIFE. Profound, isn't it? Now you know why I never answer people when they ask me where I get my ideas. Anyhow, when searching for ideas, I'm a "user." Yeah, right, I use myself. I look within my own experience to find stories that may relate to the characters I am writing for. Sitcom is based on regular characters—people you see week after week—so when you're searching for an idea for a story, find the things in yourself that you can relate to these characters and build on that foundation.

Your ideas are all about you—all about your perceptions. The life you live, the world around you, is filled with ideas for the taking. Your mind should be a "sponge," incessantly soaking up the SILLINESS, the CONTRADICTIONS, the PURELY ABSURD things that occur in REAL life. Purely absurd reality is never hard to find. Here's an example:

Lincoln's Gettysburg Address contains 266 words. The Ten Commandments, 297 words. The Declaration of Independence about 300 words. And a government order to reduce the price of cabbage contains over 26,000 words. Oh, yeah . . . Washington never ceases to be a lively source of nonsense.

Very real examples of purely absurd nonsense can also be found in these actual label instructions on consumer products:

- On a hair dryer: "Do not use while sleeping."
- On a frozen dinner: "Defrost before using."
- On a hotel shower cap: "Fits one head."
- On a string of Christmas lights: "For indoor or outdoor use only."
- On a packet of airline nuts: "Open package, eat nuts."

Keep your eyes open for little gems like these.

Write what you know about; the research is already there. Maybe it's something that happened to a friend or relative. If you have kids, there's got to be an idea for a story there somewhere. Perhaps something you read triggers a thought. Something you saw on the news. A bizarro character you observed at the airport. Always keep a pad and pencil handy so you can record your impressions. You never know when they may come in handy.

Once, in the middle of the night, I woke up and immediately wrote down a breakthrough idea. The next morning, I read what I had written, and it said, "This room smells like Rogaine." This is not to infer that I am going bald; it's just that my brain seems to be growing through my hair, and not all my breakthrough ideas are actual breakthrough ideas.

Look around. Study people. If you work for some sterile corporation, notice the pretense, the posturing. Observe how seriously most people take themselves and how they strut around as if they know what they are doing when they haven't a clue. And what's really funny is they get away with it.

Yes, people and situations are out there for us to make fun of. File your impressions in that big storage crate known as your head. Keep thinking to yourself: "I can use that someday."

NOTION PICTURES

Many of my teleplay ideas have come from my own life. In a *Happy Days* segment called "Richie's Flip Side," Richie Cunningham becomes a teen deejay at a local radio station and it goes to his head. (The big-headed deejay was me.)

During the second season of *Welcome Back, Kotter,* ego juice was flying freely among the actors and writers. Out of the flush of success, hostilities were breaking out, sides were taken, and people weren't speaking to each other. After observing this situation for a few damaging weeks, an episode called "The Fight" emerged, where a minor incident leads to the Sweathogs fighting among themselves, with Mr. Kotter playing referee. The episode turned out to be very therapeutic, and when the actors saw how ridiculously their characters were acting, it made them look at themselves, and soon enough, real-life peace was restored.

The way you perceive life is the way you process ideas. When you interpret and express an idea, it represents your own, individual experience. A good idea, thought of by you, translated into your terms, is your "voice." And, unless you have a wooden head and live with a ventriloquist, no one else has your voice. It's what makes you an individual. It's what makes you and your idea unique.

One ever-popular method for getting an idea is theft. Stealing from another source. Avoid this practice at all costs. Writers who steal are nothing but hacks with no ethics and enormous homes in Beverly Hills.

Actually, there IS a certain degree of "borrowing" in all originality. All ideas are derivative of something or someone else. I mean, where would Van Gogh be without da Vinci? Robin Williams without Jonathan Winters? Jim Carrey without Jerry Lewis? Heck, if it weren't for Mercedes, a Toyota would still look like a Toyota.

It's all the result of what we call practical education—little bits of this 'n that we've picked up from here 'n there. We keep what we like and discard the rest. Our heads are filled with this garbage. When we form ideas, we're sorting through this mental muck to put together our own, unique take on life.

ZONING OUT

In your quest for that great idea, it is never a good idea to wait around for inspiration to strike; it has to be fabricated. Personally, I've always found inspiration in second notices from the phone company.

Writing demands total concentration, intense focus. I never use the activity or the noise around me as an excuse not to work. I have the ability to completely tune out my environment, which may explain my two divorces.

In my state of aloneness, I let my mind wander (just like I used to in Economics class). I "free associate" thoughts by asking myself questions like: "What if . . . ?" or "Wouldn't it be funny if . . . ?" I challenge myself to fill in the blanks. I paint myself into a corner and try to find a way out. It gets my mind in gear, and after I stop screaming, I'm humming.

CROSS-EYED PERCEPTIONS

Successful comedy writing offers good ideas in terms of weird, offbeat perspectives on daily living. Good comedy ideas spring every which way out of conventional patterns. They slant the world at abstract angles and show it back to us through a mirror that's been dropped on its head and has a crack in it. To illustrate, here's an excerpt from a *Welcome Back, Kotter* script that I wrote with Jewel Jaffe Rannow entitled "Whodunit?":

INT. SCHOOL CORRIDOR - DAY

(IT'S MONDAY MORNING, BEFORE CLASS. STUDENTS
PASS. BARBARINO, EPSTEIN AND WASHINGTON STAND
IN THE HALL. HORSHACK <u>ENTERS</u>, A HUGE GRIN ON HIS FACE)

                    BARBARINO

          Here he is. Here's my man. How
          was your big date Saturday night?

(HORSHACK GRINS WIDER AND LAUGHS)

                    WASHINGTON

          Big date? You jivin'? Who'd go out
          with him?

                    HORSHACK

          Vinnie fixed it up.

                    BARBARINO

          Not that I wanna blow my own horn,
          but due to my stupifyin' talent with
          females of the opposite sex, I'm
          proud ta say I managed to pull off
          what the world said could never be
          pulled . . . Are ya ready? Horshack here
          went out with the one, the only,
          Rosalie Totsie!!!

```
                        ALL

        You mean "Hotsie Totsie?!"

                      EPSTEIN

        (TO HORSHACK) So tell us about Hotsie.

                     HORSHACK

        Oh—okay. Well, I borrowed my old
        man's cab and went to pick her up . . .

                    BARBARINO

        (INTERRUPTS) Would ya get to the
        good part! Did anything happen?

                     HORSHACK

        Right away—I forgot to turn off
        the "taxi" sign and we hadda take
        six people to the airport.
```

The character of Horshack is super-innocent and when we hear that "something happened" on his date with the legendary "Hotsie," we are led to an expected conclusion. We think that Horshack may have actually engaged in a virile act. Then, when we hear that he had to take six people to the airport, we are rushed back into the reality of who Horshack really is—and what a strange, oblique world he inhabits. We visualize poor Arnold being forced by six enraged people who are running late for their flight to Tallahassee. Horshack's purity and naivete always made him the ideal target for jokes, and rich story ideas.

SERIOUS HA-HA'S

Comedy is about TRAGEDY. The subject matter of most jokes, sketches, stories, columns, funny films and plays is quite serious. Getting divorced, kicked out of your apartment, fired from your job—we kid about bad news. It's like those dumb, good news/bad news jokes:

Dentist (to Patient): "I have good news and bad news. The good news is your teeth are fine. The bad news is your gums have to come out." Hey, I warned you it was dumb.

People take life and themselves entirely too seriously, and when a writer turns a serious idea into a funny one, it makes us laugh at ourselves. The more serious the situation, the more possibilities for comedy. The jokes lie in how your character perceives and reacts to the situation.

Frasier's pomposity, Larry Sanders' insecurity—these human imperfections are perfect targets for the comedy writer. The more seriously characters take themselves, the funnier they become.

One of the very best TV comedy ideas on a serious subject was the classic "Chuckles the Clown" episode of *The Mary Tyler Moore Show*. The setting is a funeral to honor the passing of TV's happy funster, Chuckles. Now, a funeral is supposed to be a serious affair, but as people recall how Chuckles used to act, Mary can't keep it in. She starts to giggle, tries to stifle it, but bursts into serious laughter. Soon everybody is hysterical at the memory of Chuckles the Clown, and I'm sure Chuckles would've wanted it that way.

FAMILIARITY BREEDS CHUCKLING

TV comedy ideas must be IDENTIFIABLE to all of us. They must elicit a reaction of "Oh, sure, that happened to me" or "that COULD happen to me."

The character of Hotsie Totsie, in *Kotter*'s "Whodunit?" could be found in every high school. She was the girl with the "reputation," whether it was deserved or not. We know this character and we can relate. Solid story ideas must have a REALISTIC base. You can't make jokes about things that are not real.

On *3rd Rock from the Sun,* Dr. Solomon (John Lithgow) and his crew are aliens. This may not be real to you, but you've been placed in their "special" world, making their bewilderment and misunderstanding about human beings a wonderfully identifiable area to hang stories and jokes on.

On the other hand, if you had once come up with an idea where Jerry Seinfeld got amnesia and became a gay Brazilian tango instructor, it wouldn't have been very realistic and probably wouldn't have sold unless it was thought up by someone on the staff and the plan had been to move the show in a different direction—like to Brazil—which never happened, not even in the final episode.

A good story idea deals with events happening all around you—dating, marriage, children, school, job, travel, politics, sex. They're all there for the taking (except for the sex).

Okay, you're thinking, I have an idea from my own life, but it might not be all that interesting to other people. No problem. If an idea based on real life doesn't seem interesting enough, EMBELLISH it. It's called DRAMATIC LICENSE. One of the real pleasures of being a writer is that you get to punch up your own life.

So, when faced with the task of thinking up an idea for a TV sitcom, there's really nothing to fear. Forget about the fact that you're expected to appeal to 80 million people. Attempting to appeal to 80 million people would take about 80 million different ideas, and that could take a big chunk out of your day.

The term "give the audience what it wants" is pure swamp water. No collective group will ever agree on what they want. It's up to you to tell them what they want. In the meantime, write for YOUR-SELF. Go with what's funny within YOU. Speak from YOUR heart. You'll be surprised at how people will listen.

There are a wealth of ideas out there waiting for your unique mark. An idea told from your own point of view—from your unique take on life—is what makes that idea "original."

KEYING IN

A good comedy story idea demands that the writer be familiar with the show and its characters. The choice is yours, so pick a show you like, one that you watch frequently. It should be a show you have an affinity for, one that reflects the type of humor you feel comfortable with. Tape it. Study the characters.

In your quest for ideas, always be aware that each show has a STAR (the focus of the piece), and most stories should be about, revolve around, or, at the very least, generate from the star.

When I worked on *Head of the Class,* a half-hour show with a cast of THIRTEEN, Howard Hesseman was the star. Howard was a true professional in his approach to his work, but he often felt that, when the show focused too much on the other actors, he wasn't being served well. It wasn't Howard's fault; the cast was simply too large. Howard left the show, and the following season the show was canceled. Never shortchange a star.

REALLY KEYING IN

I've sold a whole slew of sitcom stories because I have a METHOD that never fails. I think about the character I am featuring in my story. Frasier? Frasier's brother? His Dad? Daphne? Roz? Whoever.

I desperately attempt to find something that wasn't previously known about the character I am writing about. Some "enlightening" aspect that will cause that character to GROW in the eyes of the viewers and in the eyes of the producer I am trying to sell my idea to. It may go something like this:

"After being mugged at gunpoint, Frasier is taking Tai Kwon Do classes and converting to Buddhism."

Now, I don't know if the producers of *Frasier* would buy into this, but the possibilities are interesting and the theme (pacifism) is not a bad way to go, considering these gun-happy times we live in.

Actually, a "mugging story" might work well for a show like *3rd Rock from the Sun.* Imagine the possible reactions of this group of aliens who are struggling to understand what makes humans tick.

Look around you. Observe. Be a real sneak. Story possibilities are everywhere in your life. With practice, a good writer learns to identify these possibilities.

MASSAGING THE STORY MUSCLE

Okay, you have a great idea for your favorite show. You're committed to that idea—it's burning a hole in your brain. This is a good sign—the more friction going on between your ears, the better.

Then again, don't get carried away and start writing a script—that would be premature. It would be like smearing McDonald's special sauce on a cow while the sucker was still mooing.

Patience is required here. Diligence. You have to DEVELOP your idea into a STORY SYNOPSIS—a story with a STRUCTURE that makes it dramatically compelling. There are no different rules for comedy and drama—they both require a strong dramatic structure.

People are always coming up and telling me they have this story that I should write. (I say, "Oh, really, what is it?") And they proceed to tell me that their truck had a flat on the freeway. They stop. I prompt them to continue . . . ("Yes, and then . . . ?") They say, that's it, that's their story. When I tell them it's a mite skimpy, they reply, "Oh, you can fill in the rest. After all, you're the writer."

Well, they not only don't have a story, it's not even an idea, and it certainly isn't doable. Oh, sure, you could build on the flat tire concept, but it's not a story until you examine all the possibilities. Stories require "beats" (points of interest that keep your story interesting and move it along). These beats form a STORY STRUCTURE, and good structure requires careful nurturing.

Welcome to what is undoubtedly the most labor intensive phase of the scripting process—the development of your idea into a story.

LABOR DAZE

Your mission, should you decide to accept the consequences, is to write down your story in a page or two or three, maybe four . . . try not to make it any longer than an unabridged dictionary.

There are no set rules on how you go about writing your story. Just get to work, whether it's on a computer, a typewriter, or just a legal pad. I always begin my first writing on a legal pad or recycled paper. It's a habit from the insecurities of long ago, but it stays with me and makes me feel comfortable. It's a personal choice. Choose what makes you feel good, but be sure you always have at least TWO copies of whatever you're writing—one for your file, the other to be used as a "work copy."

I arrived late into the computer age; now I can't comprehend how I ever lived without one. I still start working in longhand, but then I enter what I've written into my computer in what amounts to a first rewrite, and in the process I've taught myself one very important lesson—SAVE CONSTANTLY. There's nothing more aggravating than accidentally erasing ten or twenty pages of comedy gold.

At this point, give yourself permission to make mistakes. All roads have bumps, and bumps often divert you toward a better path. Mistakes can point you in directions that are far better than what you had planned, so allow for surprises.

Don't be afraid to do some plain, old, rotten writing. Do not be alarmed if some of your writing seems to stink—and please don't let stink discourage you. Be aware that things that smell bad can be deceiving. I mean, if we relied strictly on smell, no one would eat cheese, so the state of Wisconsin, where I live, would not exist and the

Green Bay Packers would play their home games in Canada . . . Think about that.

THE AMUSING MUSE

Whatever you do, don't just sit there waiting for INSPIRATION to strike. Cobwebs will clog your thought gizmo. If inspiration does make an appearance, great. But most inspiration is up to you to create and only comes through ceaseless experimentation and focused thought.

Novelist John Irving had an interesting take on writing a story. He said, "I always begin with a character, or characters, and then try to think up as much action for them as possible."

Good advice. The action Irving talks about is both physical and mental—mostly, I think, mental. The action in a sitcom comes from what the characters THINK—their mental mind-sets—how they react to things. And that mentality inevitably leads to physical expression.

You have a huge advantage here. You're not starting from scratch, you're writing about already-established characters that you've seen on the tube every week. So, if your story isn't working, or you feel something is missing, play with your structure. Rewrite. Rearrange. Cut. Keep asking yourself how your character(s) would react. Have a solid idea of where you are going, what essential story beats you need to cover, and what you can easily do WITHOUT. It's imperative that you spin a good yarn.

You might try breaking your story down into brief descriptive sentences covering the important points.

This is how *Kotter's* "Whodunit" story broke down:

1. Establish Rosalie "Hotsie" Totsie's reputation when the Sweathogs brag about their exploits with her.
2. Rosalie tells Gabe Kotter she's pregnant and one of the Sweathogs is responsible.
3. Gabe tries various ways to find out who did it, and get the boy to act responsibly.
4. All the boys say they didn't do it, although Horshack wouldn't mind taking the rap.
5. Gabe confronts the Sweathogs. One of them is responsible for Rosalie's condition and he demands to know who it is.

6. One by one, the boys all deny it. Since they all denied it, Rosalie says she's not pregnant. She's cleared her name. She's a "lady."

Looks pretty easy, doesn't it? Like hell it is! For awhile I felt like sticking my head in a blender just to stop the pain. As I said, writing is hard, sometimes grueling work. This means writing and rewriting and rewriting the rewrite of your rewrites—getting your thoughts (no matter how stupid) on paper. If something isn't working, don't worry it to death; you can always go back and fix it later.

You'll likely do several revisions of your story before it's finished. If you don't need revisions you're obviously a genius, so put down this book and grab the first flight to Hollywood.

IF YOU BUILD IT, THEY WILL PAY

I'd like to give you a few TIPS that you might find useful when putting your story together. A lot of these things I learned the hard way—so thank your lucky stars you have someone like me around to help.

1. The first thing you should know when writing a story is HOW IT ENDS. The way it turns out. Once you know the ending, you have a direction to aim the story at. Without a direction, Dorothy never would have left Kansas.
2. FREE ASSOCIATE. Write down your notions at random—scene ideas, joke ideas, story elements, possible endings, whatever comes to you. Never fear to fly to bananaland. Pursue every avenue you can think of and, in the process, you'll very likely find the path you seek.
3. If you have trouble getting started, make up your own research and devise a BACK STORY that will tell you what happened to the character(s) a day, a week, even a couple of minutes before your story begins.
4. What your story is ABOUT should be established right at the top. Give an indication of what we are about to see. You only have about twenty-four minutes to tell your story, so you must grab the viewer before the viewer grabs the remote.

5. The main focus of your story will be on a specific character in the show—and you should establish that character's NEED right at the beginning of your story. This need is something the character aspires to—something that must be earned and acquired, a GOAL to be accomplished during the course of your story. It could be anything from trying to get a date to making the world safe for democracy (although the democracy goal doesn't turn up too often in your average sitcom).

You may fondly recall an episode from *Seinfeld* called "The Contest." It's the one that dealt with the ever-popular American pastime, sex without partners. The gang made a pact to see who could hold out the longest (that was their mutual GOAL). And for any fan of *Seinfeld,* you know how the contest turned out. If you're not a fan, have a little fun figuring it out for yourself.

A character's NEEDS may be conveyed in many ways. In a scene from a *Frasier* episode, Frasier's latest girlfriend has just broken up with him, and he is having a difficult time dealing with it. He is finding it impossible to achieve a sense of closure over this incident, and in true Frasier fashion, he is obsessing over the broken relationship. He can't help but wonder if there's something about HIM that caused the breakup.

Frasier's father, Martin, is put into the position of counseling his son, and he advises Frasier to stop driving himself nuts and to stop blaming himself—sometimes things can't be explained, sometimes things just happen. The way Martin sees it, Frasier has two choices: He can either forget it or spend the rest of his life torturing himself over what happened. So Frasier, of course, being Frasier, becomes determined to bolster his flagging self-confidence by getting to the bottom of this, even if it takes the rest of his life to do so.

Thus begins Frasier's quest to find out what went wrong—this is his NEED, his GOAL, and it governs his actions throughout the story. He accomplishes his goal

[Handwritten margin notes: "Goal / Obstacles / Obstacles / Conflict / Action / Overcome obstacles / Title / break story individual / scenes"]

when the girl finally admits her own fears of getting involved—Frasier's over-attention has made her see that it's time for her to commit, and if Frasier is willing, she's ready. Frasier, of course, being Frasier, shows his own fear of commitment by dumping the girl.

6. Every good script contains OBSTACLES that keep your characters from achieving their goals. It could be anything from disagreements between characters to breaking a leg or simply failing to get a job. These kinds of "twists and turns" provide CONFLICT—and conflict keeps the viewers intrigued. In *M*A*S*H*, we always knew that Major Burns would oppose Hawkeye. That's conflict, and conflict helps us structure the scenes in our story.

I recall a very funny episode of *3rd Rock from the Sun,* where Dr. Solomon is assigned an alien wife, which poses a problem since he just got engaged to Mary Albright. Solomon faces a significant obstacle by suddenly having a wife in the midst of his engagement.

7. The only way an obstacle can be overcome is through ACTION. The action the characters take—what they DO to achieve their goal, sparks the action of the story and keeps it moving ahead to its resolution.

In the same *3rd Rock from the Sun* episode, Dr. Solomon takes ACTION and cleverly devises a plan to dump his new wife by turning into a real creep. Failing in this gesture, he attempts another bold move and decides to tell his new wife the truth—that he doesn't love her. It turns out that Dr. Solomon finds it a lot easier than he thought to let his new wife down. By taking action and telling the truth, he has not only overcome HIS obstacle, he has overcome the obstacle of his wife, who thinks Dr. Solomon is a real pain.

8. The End of Act One (the Act Break) should employ a MAJOR OBSTACLE—an incident or event that complicates the character's problem and takes it to a point where the action must veer in another direction. There's a phys-

ical or emotional barrier for the character to overcome. A CLIFFHANGER situation keeps the viewers tuned-in.

A situation like this is skillfully illustrated in a scene from another *Frasier* episode, where Frasier is trying to soothe the irritable, depressive feelings of a very pregnant Roz Doyle, who sees herself as a big, fat, and unattractive.

Frasier horns in on a telephone call from Roz's mother, who is coming to visit. He tells her not to worry about her daughter—her snippy behavior is probably due to the pregnancy pounds she's been putting on.

Phone call over, Roz rejoins Frasier and apologizes to him for being such a snip. She's just nervous about her mom's upcoming visit . . . Y'see, she hasn't told her mom that she's pregnant yet.

. . . Well, you can just imagine the look on Frasier's face.

9. In Act Two, your character is overcoming an obstacle and is headed toward a RESOLUTION. In sitcom, the story usually ends happily (and hopefully surprisingly), and the problem is solved with no significant change in the character's situation. The character has likely learned a lesson, and the following week we go on as if the previous week never happened.

10. If you reach a point in your story where you don't know how your character will react to a certain situation, get personal and look into YOURSELF. How would YOU react in this situation? You are undoubtedly the best research material you have.

11. Every scene should stand on its own with a BEGIN-NING, a MIDDLE, and an END. Each scene must be ABOUT something—must have a point. Something specific should take place that reveals one element of necessary story information—information that moves the story along and retains the viewers' interest. If a scene has no point and you can do without it, do without it.

12. Many sitcoms have a major "A" STORY and a minor "B" STORY involving a different character or characters. This

is normally done to keep all the show's regular characters alive and functioning. These actors are being paid every week, so they should earn their money and stop complaining that they don't have enough time on camera. Also, the viewers should be exposed to them on a regular basis, so they get to know them. The "B" Story usually consists of one or two short scenes in each act with some kind of resolution in its final scene.

My advice is to forget writing a "B" Story in your spec script. Your job is to show the world what a great storyteller you are, so stick to that single, precious "A" Story that will be your ticket to the big show.

13. Most comedy shows use TEASERS and/or TAGS. These are usually "fluff"—joke situations that get us in and out of the episode. They should never contain important story points because they are often eliminated in syndication to make room for more commercials. So, don't worry about Teasers and Tags, just concentrate on writing a great Two-Act Story.

14. Be sensible. Always keep in mind the physical limitations of a sitcom. They are usually shot on three, possibly four INTERIOR SETS in front of a live audience, very much like a theatrical play.

I'll never forget a Story Outline I received while I was story editor on *Love, American Style*. The writer had scenes at the L.A. airport, in Dodger Stadium and on the Hollywood freeway. I've always wondered what brand of sugar that guy was sprinkling on his Wheaties.

15. And, finally, you must give your script an episode TITLE. Your title is essential to all phases of production, and can often be the seed to your entire story.

Study these fifteen TIPS. When they become second nature, you'll find that you'll have a lot more freedom to create, and you'll be well on your way to becoming an expert storyteller.

IDEAS ON A CLOTHESLINE

Congratulations, I heard that your story is great! Where did I hear it? You told me, of course. You're telling everyone! You're happy, you're proud, you've accomplished something terrific! You and your compellingly funny story are ready to go on to the next phase of the sitcom writing process—the STORY OUTLINE.

This is where you break your story down into individual SCENES. Where you write out these connected scenes into a detailed synopsis of what happens in your story. It's a story told with pictures—a continuous unfolding of circumstances and events coming to a head in a hilariously clever resolution. You can't bake a cake without a recipe, and you can't write a teleplay without an outline. It's your BLUEPRINT—a two-act, scene-by-scene progression of your story. It's a "fleshing-out" process, putting meat on the bones and adding weight to your story.

Now, if you're asking yourself what a story outline looks like, it's funny you should ask. I just happen to have the real thing—a story outline that I wrote for an episode of *Head of the Class* called "I Am The King!" I think it will serve as a very helpful example.

This is the idea I sold. Charlie Moore (Howard Hesseman) is forced to moonlight as a late night TV huckster, so he can afford a new place to live.

It's important to know that Charlie Moore is a "temporarily" failed actor who fell back on his teaching degree to make a living. Charlie teaches a history honors program at a New York City high school. His students are the best and brightest, and he works constantly to try to keep ahead of them. Here's how it went.

HEAD OF THE CLASS

"I Am The King!!"
(Story Outline)

ACT ONE

FADE IN:

1-1 INT. SCHOOL HALLWAY - DAY

Students are arriving for the day. Charlie Moore is on the pay phone. He holds the classified section of the newspaper, with various ads circled. Charlie asks if the apartment is still available? It is? What's the rent? . . . Charlie cringes and says he must have the wrong number. He quickly calls another number. The apartment is available, but they require a credit check, security deposit, cleaning fee, and first and last month's rent. Charlie quips that he shouldn't have to pay last month's rent, he didn't live there last month. They hang up on him.

1-2 INT. ADMINISTRATION OFFICE - CONTINUOUS ACTION

Charlie informs Bernadette that they're tearing down his rent-controlled building in a few weeks and he has to find another place to live. She empathizes with his problem.

Dr. Samuels enters, chuckling to himself, his face buried in an open book. Charlie can't help noticing the book's title: *How to Be Humorous For $18.95*, by Jackie Joey. Samuels explains that in his quest to be an effective educator, he has discovered humor to be the ultimate subversive tool in communication. Samuels—"The secret's in looking at life from a funny perspective. For example . . . (glances in book, tells joke) . . . If you get a little 'Gleem' in your eye, you're brushing your teeth wrong . . . Get it? Gleam? Toothpaste?"

Charlie and Bernadette just stand there, dumbfounded. Samuels tells them they've been a great audience and, in response to numerous requests, he's leaving. Samuels waits for a laugh. No laugh, so Samuels goes off laughing at his own joke.

1-3 INT. CLASSROOM - DAY

Class is in session. The kids already know about Charlie's predicament and they ask how the apartment hunting is going. Charlie reports that from what he's seen so far, apartments are going very expensively. He found one good deal, but he'd have to commute to New York City from Weiser, Idaho.

Charlie did see an apartment in the Bronx that would be perfect for him. It's this little fixer-upper, and they're not renting it, they're selling it cheap! A decent amount of money down and he could handle the monthly payments. Charlie thinks it would be nice to own a piece of land, even if it is on the sixth floor.

The class learns that Charlie leads a hand-to-mouth existence. He lives from paycheck to paycheck. He doesn't budget his money, and he has a tendency to do things like spending $300 on an antique saxophone he can't play, but looks great hanging over his bathtub.

The class wants to put Mr. Moore on a budget. Little Janice appoints herself his business manager and promises to straighten out his financial chaos for a mere commission of six percent.

Charlie insists that he can handle his own financial affairs. The class disagrees and they challenge him: If he keeps playing fast and loose with his money he'll never be able to buy that apartment. Charlie contends that there is always a way. The kids don't feel that begging would be dignified. Charlie is insulted—he would never stoop to begging.

1-4 INT. SCHOOL HALLWAY - LATER THAT DAY

Charlie is on the pay phone begging some guy named Sonny to lend him the money for a down payment on this apartment he found. The people have to sell, and they're asking a lowball price. Sonny is an old friend—a successful theatrical agent— he can afford it. Sonny has a better idea. They're casting a commercial that needs an actor of great stature and abil- ity . . . Charlie bites . . . he'll go audition. What has he got to lose?

1-5 INT. SMALL TV STUDIO - NIGHT

Charlie stands, holding a script, surrounded by home appli- ances. SID VEEMER, a 50ish man with New York in his voice is talking to Charlie. Veemer is impressed with Charlie's warmth, sincerity and comic style. Charlie's got the job. With residuals, Charlie should pick up a nice piece of change. Charlie beams, his talent has just bailed him out.

1-6 INT. CLASSROOM - A WEEK LATER

Charlie enters at the bell. The class is there. Janice notes that Mr. Moore is wearing a new tie and she'd like to have the receipt. In fact, she'd like to have all his receipts for the past week which he keeps forgetting to give her, and they should really have that talk about investing in gold futures. Charlie appreciates Janice's tenacious, never-end- ing concern for his pocketbook, but she needn't bother, his financial woes are over. The class wants to know what he did. Charlie would rather not say. It's private. He does have a personal life, you know.

Arvid tells Mr. Moore he can stop being so coy; he knows the truth. The other night, Arvid set his VCR to record the midnight movie, *How to Stuff a Wild Bikini,* and the com- mercials were almost better than the stuffed bikinis. Arvid would like to share his discovery with the class. Charlie is in traction.

Arvid turns on the classroom VCR. We SEE a 60-second spot featuring Charlie dressed as a KING in a robe, crown, even a royal scepter.

Surrounding him are home appliances of all kinds. A big sign behind him says: "VEEMER'S DISCOUNT PALACE." Charlie bolts off the throne he's sitting on and he assaults our sens- es as he does a crazed, hard-sell TV pitch, proclaiming, "I AM THE KING!!" The King of blenders, toasters, and stereos!

The class is highly amused. Charlie wishes he were in Maui.

Charlie has a midget sidekick dressed as a JESTER, who Charlie smacks in the face with the royal pie. The King blows up VCRs, smashes stereos! The King will do anything to move these appliances!

Charlie concludes by quickly telling us that Veemer's Discount Palace has thirty-two locations close to wherever you live. Open everyday until midnight. Come see the King! I AM THE KING!!

Arvid switches off the tape. The class looks at Charlie as if seeing him for the first time.

Charlie is defensive . . . the commercial was on so late . . . he didn't think they'd see it . . .

The kids rib Mr. Moore about the commercial, calling him things like Supreme Highness and Your Great Munificence. Charlie takes it good-naturedly at first, then tries to get them off the subject and into their class work, but the class can't seem to take their teacher seriously anymore. After all, he is the KING!!

FADE OUT.

END OF ACT ONE

ACT TWO

FADE IN:

2-1 INT. CLASSROOM - THE NEXT DAY

Charlie tries to teach, but the class continues to needle him about being the King. Dennis predicts he'll go down as one of the great Kings, right alongside King Kong and Burger King. Charlie rationalizes that he had to do what he had to do, and as an actor it's his duty to play the role with commitment. Veemer wanted the "hit 'em over the head" school of advertising and that's what he gave him. Charlie likes what he did. He's proud of his work.

Charlie adds that these commercials have allowed him to become a property owner. He's managed to arrange for a down payment on that little fixer-upper in the Bronx. Eric wonders if it comes with a moat, and the "King" jokes start again.

Charlie finally lays down the law—86 the King jokes, okay? Just when Charlie gets the class into the day's lesson, Dr. Samuels enters, bows low to Charlie, and beseeches his "regal loftiness" for a word with his loyal subjects. Samuels suffers from insomnia and caught Charlie's act on TV.

Samuels informs the class that he's arranged for an academic meet with Dewitt Clinton, and he knows they can't lose because their teacher is the King! Samuels waits for the laugh. The kids try very hard to keep straight faces. Samuels shrugs and exits laughing at his own quip, and saying, "What a crowd, what a crowd."

Now that they're on the subject of royalty again, the class wants to know how many more commercials they can look forward to seeing? Charlie explains that he signed to do four spots: He's already done three and he's shooting the last one after school. The class wants to go with him and see how a commercial is made. It would be very educational, like attending a coronation, or at least a Prince concert.

Charlie wavers, then, speaking as the King, he grants his vassals their divine request.

2-2 INT. SMALL TV STUDIO - LATER THAT DAY

The class is there to watch Mr. Moore tape his commercial. Charlie (dressed as the King) shows his subjects around "this most amazing spot which he calls Camelot."

Alan is chatting with the midget Jester who is a member of Actors Studio, and is hoping to play in *Death of a Salesman* at Lincoln Center with an all-short cast.

Sid Veemer appears and instructs the King and the Jester to take their places—it's time to make movies! Charlie goes into his frantic spiel, announcing a "King-Sized Sale" on refrigerators! The rehearsal goes perfectly. Veemer says they'll go for a take. Action!

Charlie begins, forgets a line, and ad-libs something funny for the kid's benefit. The kids laugh.

Veemer cuts and asks if the peanut gallery would refrain from laughing. Charlie assures Veemer his little peanuts will be as quiet as mice. The kids all nod and squeak like mice. Veemer shakes his head and calls for take two.

2-3 SAME SCENE - LATER

Charlie is flawlessly running through a take. He swings open the refrigerator door, then mixes up his next line, so it makes no sense at all. Veemer cuts. Charlie apologizes. Veemer calls for another take.

2-4 SAME SCENE - LATER

Charlie gets all his lines right, but at the end, the refrigerator door sticks and Charlie struggles to open it. The kids laugh. Veemer cuts. Let's do it again.

2-5 SAME SCENE - LATER

Charlie is giving a flawless performance, the refrigerator door opens easily, but at the end the Jester misses Charlie with his seltzer bottle, schpritzing Veemer instead. The kids love it. Veemer shoots them a look and they squeak like mice again. Veemer suggests they try it once more for accuracy.

2-6 SAME SCENE - LATER

The Jester schpritzes Charlie and they conclude a perfect take. That's a print! The kids applaud. Charlie responds with a courtly bow to his public.

The kids gather around as Veemer tells Charlie that their TV campaign has taken off much bigger than expected. He wants Charlie to sign on for six more spots, which will include personal appearances at his stores all over the city, including Jersey. He'll be a full-time potentate.

Charlie glances at the kids, tells Veemer he can't do that, he teaches school. Veemer tells him to quit—a King makes a lot more than a teacher. Charlie supposes that's true. He looks at the intent faces of his class.

The kids, figuring Charlie will go for the money, do pointed jokes denying that they would feel betrayed, even though he's stabbing them in their young, impressionable backs . . . But, hey, it's not their decision, only Mr. Moore can decide what he wants to be when he grows up.

Charlie has an idea and he requests one more take of the commercial . . . This time, he ad-libs a brand-new ending where the refrigerator sale is so astounding that it is KILLING the King! Charlie clutches his heart, gasps, and falls to the floor, dead.

Veemer cuts—asks Charlie what he thinks he's doing?
Charlie announces that his reign is over. He's sorry (boy,
is he sorry) but the King is dead. Long live the teacher.

2-7 INT. CLASSROOM - NEXT MORNING

Class is in session. Charlie is reflecting on his brief flir-
tation with fame. He got an apartment and half-off on a
refrigerator. What more could a dead monarch ask for?

Dr. Samuels enters, informs the class that the bus for
their academic meet at Dewitt Clinton will be leaving sharply
after school on Friday. Be on it!

Charlie waits for the inevitable joke. No joke. Samuels
has decided to forget the humorous approach. No one appre-
ciated it. He was the only one laughing. His wife got so fed
up she put his joke book in the blender and poured it over
his spaghetti. Charlie laughs—now THAT'S funny. Samuels says
it's no laughing matter and exits.

Arvid has a surprise for Mr. Moore. He taped the late
movie again last night and thought they might like to see
the commercial.

Arvid plays the tape which now features Sid Veemer as
the NEW appliance King, announcing a "Memorial Sale" on
microwaves in honor of the deceased King. "The King is dead
—I am the NEW king!!"

Charlie finds comfort in knowing that his death was not
in vain.

FADE OUT.

END OF ACT TWO

And, so, Charlie Moore walks off into the Manhattan sitcom sunset
secure in the fact that his commitment to being a teacher is stronger
than ever . . .

Any comments on this outline? I have one. I think it sucks. It
misses the mark completely. It takes a good idea and doesn't do a
whole lot with it. I failed to tell the story in an interesting and compelling way. Study it. See if you agree with what I am saying.

This is no joke. I'm serious. Other writer/teachers will always
show you their best work, to give the impression they never make

mistakes. Well, I don't teach that way. I make mistakes all the time, and I want you to take an active part in my quest.

It's been years since I wrote this outline, and I have come back to it with a new perspective. In retrospect, I have become my own worst critic. Looking at this outline from a distance of time, I can't help thinking, "Who wrote this crap?"

I was far from a beginning writer when I wrote this crap. I had written over one hundred story outlines by this time in my career, as well as revising the outlines of others as a staff writer and producer. Some of my outlines were fairly easy to write; others, like "I Am the King," were white-knucklers. These babies are never a snap to turn out.

Each story idea has its own life—its own unique demands and built-in problems. No TV writer—no writer in the world—ever becomes an absolute expert on storylines. Each writing project is a new challenge. With experience, you get more skilled at critiquing the work of others, but when it comes to your own "baby," you can lose your objectivity along the way.

The "I Am the King" story outline you have just read shows you the descriptive PROSE form that is used to illustrate the action in each scene, with a few jokes thrown in. And although this outline is a tad on the long side, there's fun stuff in there. (I always liked the kids squeaking like mice.)

But I was wandering—trying to hook into a story that was eluding me. The show's producers were in a hurry for my outline. I felt rushed, and my mind turned into temporary tofu. What I had settled on lacked the proper dramatic thrust. Some scenes weren't the right scenes. Many story points went nowhere, and the ending just sort of happened in a "so what, he decided to remain a teacher" fashion. (Maybe Charlie should've gone for the money. I could have gotten a two-parter out of it.)

The ending was always a problem; I hadn't given it enough thought and I pretty much stumbled my way to a conclusion. I really wasn't committed to where I was going and a story must always have a definite direction in order to be told effectively. A good story has to have an interesting PLOT.

THE PLOT THICKENS

This will be a short chapter—but probably the most important chapter in this book—it's all about PLOT.

Plot. Funny word, isn't it? It sounds like the gooey stuff your dog just dripped all over your new white sneakers. The dictionary defines plot as "a small place of burial," but that may not be the definition we are looking for. The dictionary goes on, however, to tell us that plot is "the plan or main story of a composition—a flow of events or happenings that constitute the action of a narrative or drama." Or, in our case, a comedy.

A plot is a well-crafted plan—a sequence of happenings that provide intrigue, intensity, and surprise. It makes your story so compelling that the audience can't wait to see how it's going to end. If you're reading a novel you can't put down, it's because it has a good plot (or maybe lots of naked scenes).

TV viewers watch shows like *Murder, She Wrote* and *Diagnosis, Murder* for the plot. They watch *Newsradio* and *Just Shoot Me* for the plot with laughs. Even rugrats watch *Rugrats* for the plot.

Your plot is the "backbone" of your teleplay story. In my "I Am the King" outline, I had a plot—it just wasn't put together in a very interesting way. No writer should ever begin outlining a teleplay story (or engage in any fiction writing) without a preconceived plot worked out. Ignoring this would be like taking an around-the-world trip on a skateboard.

There is no set formula for plotting a story, but there are "principles" to be adhered to. And you must fully understand these principles before you can even think about writing to sell. Once these principles are set in your mind, you are free to have fun, entertain, and buy a BMW.

A good plot has FOUR COMPONENTS:

1. A PREMISE. Your story has to be well-defined. It should address a subject—be about something. It's imperative that you know from the start what it is you're writing about. My problem in the "I Am the King" outline was that I never really had a grasp of what I was writing about. I had a good idea, ran with it, and ended up nowhere.

2. A solid plot has to be INTERESTING. Complications and a hefty helping of confusion add interest to a comedy plot. So does suspense. Some jeopardy. The unexpected. You have to get viewers so involved that they are incapable of flipping the channel to "Squirrel Huntin' With Farmer Bob."

3. An effective plot has to be BELIEVABLE and, as a humorist, it is your job to s-t-r-e-t-c-h reality. Be as silly and as over the top as you can be, as long as your story makes sense. The entrance of a new character at the end who saves the day is junk writing. Things have to happen for a reason.

4. An interesting plot has PLOT POINTS. These are the story "beats" I have previously referred to. A plot point is when some event takes place that "twirls" the story around in another direction. It's a twist—a turn that is unpredictable, intriguing, and that causes new action and new development. A plot point raises the stakes, propels the story forward; it's the fuel that allows the vehicle to keep going.

Good examples of plot points are found in *Welcome Back, Kotter's* "Whodunit":

1. In the first scene, the boys (Sweathogs) brag about being intimate with Rosalie "Hotsie" Totsie, the girl with the reputation. This sets up the plot.
2. Rosalie tells Mr. Kotter she is pregnant, and one of the Sweathogs did it. This is a plot point that swings the whole story into action.
3. When the Sweathogs are evasive (plot point), Mr. Kotter is bent on finding out who's responsible (plot point). This strengthens Kotter's resolve and propels the action forward.
4. When the boys all deny that they've ever been close to Rosalie, the plot takes a major twist.
5. In a final plot turn, Rosalie admits the truth. She's not pregnant; she just wanted to clear her reputation.

LEAVE THE DRIVING TO FRASIER

You've heard the phrase "character-driven." Well, character-driven is a sitcom plot that is driven by the character(s). (Hey, what can I say? Profundity is my middle name.)

The simple fact is that characters are not "types," they are human beings. And you are writing about human beings for the entertainment of human beings, so your plot depends on the HUMAN ELEMENT—the struggles of your characters to satisfy their "need."

You establish a dramatic premise when the characters find themselves in a predicament. Then complications heighten the predicament, building to a climax, then to a solution. These circumstances provide the character with the motivation to move on. This generates action and action generates plot.

If Frasier falls in love and then gets cold feet and ends up jilting the woman, it's an intriguing idea, but it's not a plot. HOW Frasier falls and, especially, HOW he manages to jilt his new-found love— that is a plot. The intricacies, incidents, unexpected twists—the actions he takes—all combine to build plot.

GRAB 'EM AND DON'T LET GO

Your plot has one major purpose—to hold the interest of the TV viewer (or in the case of your "spec" script, the fascination of the reader).

True, there are writers who begin their stories without a worked-out plot, but these are experienced writers who are very familiar with the principles of plotting. They have a goal in sight. They very likely know where they are headed, and they are fully aware that their story will grow naturally through their character's relationships and objectives. Despite my past experience, I am NOT that kind of experienced writer. Whenever I fly blindly, I am Wile E. Coyote, headed smack into the nearest cliff. So, heed my warning.

It is imperative that you have some idea of your plot before you begin writing a script. This is where I screwed up with the "I Am the King" outline. The plotting was shoddy because I didn't address it strongly enough in the story stage. If I had taken more time, given it more thought, I would have written a much better story outline, and could've saved myself the trouble of smacking into that stupid cliff.

Time has allowed me to understand the journey that "I Am the King" took before it reached the cameras. I was just emerging from a "valley" phase of a career filled with hills and valleys, and I was fighting like hell to get back on top. *Head of the Class* was a hot, new show and, although I was mired in doubt and anxiety, I wanted to do a great job and impress. So, did I impress? Keep reading.

"I AM THE KING" REVISITED

When I arrived at the *Head of the Class* production offices for notes on my outline, I found that my sneakiest suspicions were confirmed. The producers were disappointed with my treatment of what they still felt was a great idea.

At first, I was hurt, I was defensive, and I was experiencing one of the most important lessons of TV writing—the realization that there actually are other intelligent people in this world who can help you with your work. This experience begins with what is called CRITICISM, and how you handle this criticism will affect your entire career.

There is a popular belief among writers: We know everything about our writing and have a complete mastery of our subject, so don't you dare change a word or idea. This can be a foolish belief in sitcom writing because sitcom is very much a COLLABORATIVE medium. When you buy into the business, you buy into that.

A writer deeply engrossed in developing a story idea often lacks the objectivity to see alternative ways of telling the story, but the critique of another writer (one you trust) may give you insights into your story that may not have occurred to you.

Now, I'm not saying you should lay down, play dead, and be a "yes" person. Those jobs are all filled in Hollywood. Stick up for what you firmly believe in! Always be prepared to defend your ideas, but remain open-minded and perceptive enough to recognize something better when it is offered to you. A good writer is a good LISTENER.

During the critiquing of "I Am the King," my years of experience had equipped me with the ability to recognize when someone else's idea was a better idea. The decision of whether to accept or reject new ideas was clearly up to me, and I was smart enough to know that I should never let my ego get in the way. It wasn't me, the writer, who was being served here—it was the writing itself.

THE STORY IS ALL

Nobody writes anything completely alone. Even Ernie Hemingway and Scotty Fitzgerald had editors who aided them through the story process. Margaret Mitchell was saved from embarrassment when her editor suggested she change the title of her story from *Scarlett Eats a Carrot* to *Gone with the Wind* . . . and that's a fact.

In the case of "I Am the King," the producers' criticism wasn't cruel, nor was it too specific (that is, I received no ultimatums telling me to change certain things or else). The general feeling was that the outline could have a better STRUCTURE to make it more interesting to the TV audience. It was decided that the story needed more analysis—more experimentation. I hadn't asked myself "What if . . .?" or "Wouldn't it be funny if . . .?" often enough.

I even added other questions that could evoke curious results—questions such as, "What's the silliest, most surprising thing that could happen?" "How else might the character react?" "Who else might get involved to help or hinder the situation?" "What are valuable things we do not yet know about these characters?" The answers to questions like these led me closer to my goal. There were a million possible ways this story could be told, and I had to find the one best suited to me. I also had to find a much better ending.

As the producers gave me my notes for the "I Am the King" outline, I felt energized. I had hurriedly settled on a story direction that I must admit I wasn't even sure of myself (a grave error), but now I was excited at the prospect of making it better. I was still in control of my own story. I had been reprieved!

WAYS AND MEANS

The first thing I did was to go back and rethink my story synopsis. Then, as I wrote the revised outline, I found that I began to "free associate" more and let new, fresh ideas for scenes come to me.

Now, this is going to sound extremely spiritual or downright whacko, but I've always believed that stories are already written— they're drifting out there in the cosmos and it's up to us to concentrate, open up our minds, and "channel" these stories onto the page. You will never get results without intense focus and concentration. If you don't open your mind, you can't expect anything to fall out onto the paper.

As I chugged full-steam into my rewrite, I wrote the scene ideas that came to me on separate 3×5 cards, along with brief notes about what takes place in each scene. I arranged the cards on the floor. Some tack them to a bulletin board, but I prefer working on my knees (the humbling effect makes me work harder). I repeatedly rearranged the cards that I had arranged, and when I discovered "holes" in the story, I wrote more cards. I added, discarded, and continued to free associate new ideas.

I kept my focus on new possibilities for Act One and Act Two endings as I fearlessly experimented, never afraid to make mistakes. After all, they were private mistakes—no one would ever see them—and, as I've said before, mistakes can often lead you amazing, off-the-wall places.

An alternative to the 3×5 cards is a method I sometimes use where you write down whatever comes into your head, in no particular order. (Once again, you are free-associating.) Then you "cut and paste," arranging and rearranging your thoughts until a real story begins to take shape from your idea. Nowadays, this method can be employed on a computer if you've gotten to the point where you have figured out how the heck your computer works.

In this instance, I chose the card method and, as the cards fell into place, the scenes began to tell Charlie Moore's story in a very different way:

HEAD OF THE CLASS

"I Am the King!!"
(Revised Story Outline)

ACT ONE

FADE IN:

1-1 INT. HALLWAY - MORNING

Arvid is struggling to load large pieces of lumber into his locker. He tells Eric and Darlene that he is taking woodshop class to prove that he can work with his hands as well as his head. He's making a computer console with a color monitor compartment, a pull-out printer stand, and a storage module for floppies and accessories. Eric and Darlene think it's terrific that Arvid is taking woodshop. What has he learned so far? Arvid—"How to untangle my shirt from the drill press."

SCENE NOTE: Okay, you're probably saying, "he tells me not to worry about a 'B' Story, and here he is starting with a "B" story in his stupid outline." Well, I still say you should only concentrate on telling an "A" story in your "spec" script. Besides, in my case, this was a script about to be produced, and I was a writer with credentials, so just shut up and keep reading.

Anyhow, the "B" Story themes of Janice taking over Charlie's finances and Samuels's attempts at being funny were not working in the first outline. I never developed them beyond the category of bits (or "runners" as they are called in comedy writing). So, anyhow, I decided to open with a "B" Story idea I had been kicking around for awhile—wimpy Arvid Engen takes shop. In this very first scene, any perceptive writer worth his noodles can see where this is going, and it promises to be a fun trip.

1-2 INT. CLASSROOM - DAY

The bell rings. Charlie walks into class and dumps the con-
tents of a paper bag on his desk—a pot, a pan, beads, and
cheap jewelry. Charlie is in a surly mood as he bitterly
relates the familiar story of how the Dutch bought Manhattan
from the Indians for $24 worth of junk.

Charlie tells the class that, to the Indians, the land
belonged to the people and people were part of the land, so
they had a tough time understanding the European concept of
land ownership. Basically, the Indians got screwed, which set
the tone for all future real estate transactions in New York
City. The little people are being squeezed out by the high
rollers.

The class deduces that Mr. Moore is having real estate
problems of his own. Charlie tries to evade the issue, then
finally admits that his apartment building is going co-op.

SCENE NOTE: This scene sets up the story in a much more
illustrative way. Charlie Moore is put into a good light as
a history teacher because he channels his distress into a
demonstrative and creative teaching exercise. Also, the idea
of his building going "co-op" is a much better plot point
than my old idea of tearing it down. We leave the scene knowing that Charlie has a problem . . . and what that problem
could be holds the audience's interest.

1-3 INT. ADMINISTRATION OFFICE - LATER THAT DAY

Charlie shows Bernadette and Dr. Samuels a letter he received
from his landlord. His building is going co-op and he has
the option of buying his apartment, but the minimum down payment is a little maximum for minimum. Charlie's been looking
for another apartment, but there doesn't seem to be anything
he can afford that includes indoor plumbing.

Samuels urges Charlie to buy the apartment. If he doesn't
go for this deal, it'll be the dumbest thing he ever did in
his life, and Samuels assumes that Charlie has done a lot of
dumb things. Samuels exits.

Charlie wonders aloud to Bernadette . . . he's always
seen himself as the strong, silent "drifter" type. Maybe it's
time for him to make a long-term commitment. Bernadette hopes
he'll decide soon; according to the landlord's letter, he
starts drifting next Tuesday.

SCENE NOTE: This scene has levels of action. It explains Charlie's "need" (plot point). It shows his emotional reaction, and sets him to thinking that he just may be able to do something about his situation. When reminded of "Tuesday," he is pushed closer to action. The mention of Tuesday also puts a time limit, or a "clock," on the story. Something must be accomplished before a certain time or else. (This "clock" was lacking in the first outline). The exact amount of down payment is purposely never mentioned. Let the audience imagine their own amount. This way the viewer participates. It's interactive.

1-4 INT. HALLWAY - CONTINUOUS ACTION

Charlie comes out of the Administration Office and goes directly to the pay phone, passing Arvid, Maria, Jawaharlal, and Simone at Arvid's locker.
    Arvid is showing his classmates a crude, unpainted coffee table. It's made of solid bird's eye maple and he'll be able to use it once he gets the legs even. Arvid was going to make a computer console, but his band-saw had other ideas, and before he knew it he was knee-deep in kindling.

ANGLE - CHARLIE ON PHONE

Charlie is talking to Tony, his acting agent. He needs bucks fast, so he's resorting to his God-given acting talent. And although his roots are in the classical theatre, he will consider doing commercials. Something with dignity—E.F. Hutton, American Express, Grey Poupon . . .

SCENE NOTE: CONTINUOUS ACTION means just that—the action continues from the previous scene. A "B" Story scene and an "A" Story scene are combined here in the Hallway to give the scene a flow. We follow Arvid's progress in woodshop. We see that Charlie has indeed decided to do something about his living situation (plot point). Charlie's agent's name has gone from "Sonny" to "Tony" for no apparent reason. I think one of the show's producers made this change because he had a rich uncle Tony he was trying to suck up to.

1-5 INT. APPLIANCE STORE - NIGHT

Charlie stands, holding a script, amid home appliances—dish-
washers, refrigerators, stereos, VCR's, ranges. He has a big
grin on his face.
    SID VEEMER, the store owner, and RICH MICHAELS, a young
ad exec, tell Charlie he got the job. They compliment
Charlie's fabulous face. "Look at that face." "It's an
Everyman face." "A gold face." "A face you can trust." They
want to sign him for six commercials to start, with more to
follow. Charlie's delighted, but a bit apprehensive. He wonders exactly when these commercials will be on the air. Would
a lot of people see them? Veemer is sorry, but he can only
afford to air them after midnight, during the old movies.
Charlie doesn't mind. Night people. Very smart move.

SCENE NOTE: An important plot point—Charlie got the job. It
has something to do with selling appliances, and it looks
like Charlie will make some money. This new approach to the
scene shows Charlie's cautious attitude about the situation.
Although he doesn't come right out and say it, he seems to
be worried that the kids and other people at school will see
him on TV. His snobbish, theatrical friends would look down
on his commercialism. This is never said—it's called "sub-
text." As a writer you must get inside the head of your character and know what he is thinking, how he is feeling, and
reflect these things in dialogue. Charlie is relieved that
the commercials will air after midnight. But why?

1-6 INT. CLASSROOM - MORNING

Class is in session. Continuing his lesson, Charlie tells the
class about Chief Sitting Bull's speech at the completion of
the Union Pacific Railroad. In the Sioux language, Sitting
Bull told the crowd how much he hated white people, called
them thieves and liars for stealing tribal land. But the
translator cleaned it up and the Chief got a standing ova-
tion. Sitting Bull was so popular he ended up as the star of
Buffalo Bill's Wild West Show.
    The class thinks Sitting Bull sold out. Charlie is defen-
sive; he disagrees. Sitting Bull wanted to become a public
figure, so he could help his people hold on to what little

land they had left. When you only have a little space of your own, you realize it's terribly important to you.

The class appreciates what Mr. Moore is saying, but they still think Sitting Bull sold out—he went for the money. Charlie says that selling out is not just about money, it's about losing your integrity.

The BELL RINGS. As the class starts to file out, they ask Mr. Moore how his apartment situation is going. Charlie says he thinks he's going to try to buy his apartment. The class wonders how he will do that. Charlie is suddenly defensive. He never should have brought his personal situation into the classroom. Everything's okay—okay?!

SCENE NOTE: Charlie continues to relate his personal situation in the class lesson. This required research on my part, but I've always loved doing research. Besides, this is a show about smart kids and Charlie Moore's lessons must contain information that even these budding geniuses may have overlooked. (This educational aspect is totally missing from the first outline.) This classroom scene also keeps the class alive in the story, which must be done because we leave the kids and the school when we go to the appliance store.

The main plot point here is that Charlie has decided to try to buy his apartment. When the class challenges Charlie on the issue of selling out, it makes Charlie ill-at-ease and he gets defensive. This becomes intriguing. What is there about these commercials that has Charlie worried?

You may have noticed that in this scene terms like "class thinks" and "class appreciates" are used. This is only shorthand. A "class" can't do anything unless each member participates individually. So when you see these terms being used they indicate lines (hopefully jokes) from various class members. It's a large cast, so you try to give everyone their "moment."

1-7 INT. ADMINISTRATION OFFICE – AFTERNOON

Bernadette tells Charlie that a Mr. Veemer from the appliance store called and his first commercial will be airing tonight. Bernadette's excited that Charlie is going to be on TV. Now he can buy his place!

Charlie is secretive. He'd like to keep a low profile about this. Bernadette promises that no one else will know. Charlie's grateful. Bernadette (smiles impishly): "Of course, *I'LL* know."

SCENE NOTE: Charlie is found out. We learn that the commercials are about to go on the air (plot point), which heightens Charlie's anxiety about being found out by everyone.
Charlie commits Bernadette to secrecy. What is he hiding?

1-8 DENNIS'S BEDROOM - NIGHT

The lights are off. Dennis is sitting up in bed, scarfing a
huge bowl of popcorn. His face is illuminated by the light
of the TV, as he intently watches an old monster flick.

ANGLE ON TV SCREEN

We see the tail end of an unidentifiable black and white hor-
ror movie scene. CUT TO commercial and we are:

INT. APPLIANCE STORE - NIGHT (ON TV SCREEN)

A sign reads "VEEMER'S DISCOUNT PALACE." We see APPLIANCES of
all kinds. A small man dressed as a COURT JESTER holds up a herald trumpet, blows an off-key fanfare and announces "THE KING!"
    A curtain parts, revealing Charlie seated on a throne,
dressed in a robe and crown, waving a royal scepter. "The
King is here! I am the King!"

SHOT - DENNIS

In shock over what he is seeing.

BACK TO TV SCREEN

Charlie bolts off the throne and assaults our senses as he
launches into a rapid-fire, hard-sell TV pitch.

SHOT - DENNIS

Dennis scrambles across his bed to get to the phone. He calls
Eric and tells him to turn on channel 7 quick!

BACK TO TV SCREEN

Charlie will do anything to give you an imperial bargain! He
has the Jester smack himself in the face with the royal cream

pie. Charlie declares "war" on high prices, and swings his scepter, smashing a VCR into pieces.

SHOT - DENNIS

Dennis tells Eric to call the girls, he'll call the boys. This great moment in media is not to be missed.

BACK TO TV SCREEN

The Jester blows another off-key fanfare. Charlie grabs the herald trumpet, puts it to his lips and plays like Louis Armstrong. Charlie winks at the camera and says, "The King can do anything! Now back to our movie."

FADE OUT.

END OF ACT ONE

SCENE NOTE: First, Dennis's Bedroom is a one-time only SET, which meant it had to be specially built, and it shows how the character of Dennis spends his evenings. This was a much better way for me to end Act One, although I would not recommend adding new sets in your spec script.

In the first outline, I was never really sold on Arvid bringing the videotape into the classroom. It lacked drama. This scene is cinematically divided between Dennis and what Dennis is seeing on TV. It reveals to Dennis what Charlie is up to (plot point). It tells us that all the class members are now going to know what Mr. Moore's been hiding. Charlie has been discovered. This Act Ending leaves the viewer wondering what kind of reactions Charlie is in for.

ACT TWO

FADE IN:

2-1 INT. CLASSROOM - DAY

The class is gathered around Charlie's desk discussing his royal debut on late-night TV.

Charlie enters ready to begin class. Eric has an important question about movies. If Mr. Moore had a choice, which video would he rent—*King Of Kings, The King and I*, or *The Man Who Would Be King?* The class continues: *King Kong, King Rat, King Lear.* Suddenly, it hits Charlie. He's uneasy, so he chimes in with a few of his own: King Crab, Burger King, B.B. King!

Charlie's embarrassed—his secret is out—they saw him on TV, huh? They probably think he sold out. The class is amazingly supportive. They respect Mr. Moore for doing what he had to do. They also think he did a wonderful acting job—he played a deranged King and they all agree he was hopelessly deranged.

Charlie is pleased with their support. He's really having fun playing the King, and the gig has enabled him to save for the down payment on his palace. In fact, he just signed to do more commercials. The class chants, "Long live the King!" Charlie beams.

SCENE NOTE: In the first outline, Act Two begins with Charlie already knowing that his students saw him on TV. There's no surprise. This new approach allows us to see Charlie get caught. The first short paragraph in this scene translates into pages as each member of the class gets to do jokes about their teacher, "King Charles of Moore."

The jokes take the edge off and Charlie seems to become more at ease with being discovered. A delightful curve is thrown and Charlie's worst fears are dashed when the class supports what he is doing. He didn't sell out! Charlie is now a confident King.

The Story seems over at this point. Charlie is close to achieving his goal. Or is there yet another "obstacle" around the corner . . . ?

2-2 INT. HALLWAY - AFTER CLASS

It's between classes. The usual flow of student traffic through the halls. Arvid, wood chips on his shirt and sawdust on his glasses, is about to put a 12" × 18" piece of wood in his locker.

Sarah and Janice appear and Arvid shows them his solid bird's eye maple breadboard. They thought he was making a coffee table. Arvid says he was, but by the time he got the legs leveled it was only three inches high, so he decided to convert it into a lazy susan. But then he couldn't find the "off" switch on his power chisel . . .

SCENE NOTE: We're back to the progression of our "B" story. If you haven't guessed by now, Arvid's project will continue to get smaller.

At the top of the scene, I suggested "student traffic." This is helpful to the production team, who can plan to hire extras. Never be afraid to briefly describe the scene as you see it.

I bring in various members of the class to Arvid's locker during this story. I figure these kids don't have a whole lot to do in this episode, so if I give them a great line or a moment, they'll look forward to coming to work that week. Actors are competitive and they fight like hell to get their time on camera.

Also, although this is a machine shop story, notice that we never go to the machine shop. There's no need to. Producers always hire writers who think economically.

2-3 INT. DR. SAMUELS' OFFICE - DAY

Charlie has been called in for a meeting with Dr. Samuels. Samuels wants Charlie to know that he has nothing against moonlighting. A lot of teachers work second jobs, but Charlie's job is too visible. Personally, Samuels doesn't care if Charlie wants to go on TV and act like a buffoon, but the members of the Board don't feel as charitable about this. Seeing one of the teachers of the Honors Program hawking waffle irons on the tube makes them very unhappy. Samuels orders Charlie to give up his throne.

Charlie will not be pushed around. Playing the King is going to pay for his castle. So unless the Board members want to give him a hefty raise, he is going to stay the King. Charlie exits, declaiming "I Am the King!"

SCENE NOTE: At this point in the first outline, I had nowhere to go with the story and I drifted off into a scene with the class watching Charlie shoot his commercial. Big mistake. The scene did nothing to move the story forward. This new approach kept the story compelling with fresh elements. Samuels has ordered Charlie to drop the "King" bit (plot point) and Charlie is resisting and putting his job at risk. A new "obstacle" has appeared. Another strong plot point. These plot points keep the story healthy and alive. The viewer has definitely put down the remote control.

2-4 INT. APPLIANCE STORE - NIGHT

A CREW is setting up to shoot a commercial. Charlie (dressed as the King) sweeps into view. He has a lot of new angles on the King's character and he can't wait to try them out.

Sid Veemer tells Charlie there's a problem. This is going to be their last commercial. Veemer appreciates what Charlie has done, but he's too far in debt, so he's filed for Chapter 13 bankruptcy and he's liquidating everything.

Charlie is sad to hear that, but he wants Veemer to know that, because of him, he's been able to buy his apartment.

As a housewarming gift, Veemer gives Charlie a free refrigerator. Better him than a liquidator. In fact, Charlie should take TWO. Charlie doesn't know what he's going to do with two refrigerators. Veemer tells him he's a clever guy, he'll think of something.

Charlie goes on camera and announces the "Sale of the Century!" These bargains are unbelievable! The King can't stand it! It's killing the King! The King is dying! The King . . . is dead! Charlie clutches his heart and falls to the floor in a heap.

SCENE NOTE: An unexpected twist. Veemer is going belly up (plot point). I have always had, and still do have, a little bit of trouble with this turn in the story. It was a way out, and thinking of nothing better, I took it. This bankruptcy thing came out of the blue. I know life is like that, but I'm still not happy. Sue me, I'm a very picky person.

What I AM happy with is Charlie's way of handling the situation (plot point). His inventive mind gives "Veemer's Discount Palace" the kind of dramatic and funny send-off people will never forget. I mean, when's the last time you saw a King die on TV? Also, a gift of two free refrigerators could have an unexpected payoff.

2-5 INT. CLASSROOM - NEXT DAY

Charlie, wearing his crown and holding his scepter, is quoting Shakespeare's "Richard II" to the class.

"I give this heavy weight from off my head (TAKES OFF CROWN) and this unwieldy scepter from my hand (LAYS DOWN SCEPTER). The pride of kingly sway from out my heart. All pomp and majesty, I do forswear." The class applauds. Mr.

Moore will always be King to them. The memory of him in that stupid crown won't be easy to forget.

Charlie is joyous. Today he signs the deed to his apartment—that most congenial spot that he calls Camelot. Dennis corrects him—"You mean "Costalot."

Dr. Samuels peeks in the door, asks Charlie if he could have a word with him in the hall.

SCENE NOTE: Howard Hesseman, who played Charlie Moore, loved this scene. How often does a sitcom star get to do Shakespeare? Be nice to your star: He is the reason writers are working. It's his face on the screen every week, not yours. Pleasing the star might be reason enough to do this scene, but we also learn that Charlie is signing the deed (plot point). It's official. He has accomplished his goal—satisfied his NEED.

2-6 INT. HALLWAY - CONTINUOUS ACTION

Samuels thanks Mr. Moore for getting the Board off his back. It was very clever the way Charlie committed suicide on television. Charlie says it was the least he could do. It looks like Samuels owes him one, huh? Samuels guesses he does. And, as Charlie begins to sell Samuels a brand-new refrigerator at a rock-bottom price, Samuels looks trapped.

SCENE NOTE: Charlie is officially off the hook and Samuels thinks he did it to save him. Charlie plays along. He has an extra, free refrigerator. Why not sell it to a grateful and captive audience like Dr. Samuels? It made for an amusing and tidy conclusion.

2-7 INT. HALLWAY - END OF SCHOOL DAY

Charlie is leaving for the day. Arvid is at his locker. He spots Charlie and limps over to him. Arvid's limping because of a shop accident. The hammer missed his thumb and hit his foot. Arvid made Mr. Moore a housewarming gift—a single solid bird's eye maple bookend. If Mr. Moore likes it, he'll get some more bird's eye maple and start on the other one. Charlie loves the bookend, tells Arvid to go ahead and get to work on its mate. Arvid just stands there, in absolute terror.

FADE OUT.

SCENE NOTE: This is an apt close to the "B" Story. Just when
Arvid thinks his problem is finally over, his generosity puts
him right back into a situation he can't possibly handle.

END OF ACT TWO

THE END

Now, I don't know about you, but I think this revised outline brought
me a helluva lot further along on my journey toward readying this
piece of work for the tube. I now had a more substantial "blueprint"
upon which I was ready to build my script.

By the way, in case you're wondering why the producers
bought this story in the first place, I have a few theories:

1. The situation is ripe for jokes, and the star, Howard
   Hesseman, had a legitimate reason to dress up silly and act
   crazy.
2. The theme itself is universal. It's about having a place to
   live—a basic human "need" that hits a certain nerve in people, and that is the essence of successful TV sales.

"I Am the King" ain't exactly *Shakespeare in Love* but, what the hey, it
made me good money and when it aired it achieved high ratings in
both first run and rerun. Good ratings encourage advertisers to buy
time and, in TV, that's the name of the game.

WRITER'S BLOCK

A story synopsis and the subsequent story outline are not easy to exe-
cute well. They require intense concentration and experimentation,
and many believe that they cause that well-known bugaboo "writer's
block."

If you claim to have this affliction, I have no sympathy for
you. I don't give a flying fandango how you feel today. Your subcon-
scious is waiting to be let out for a walk, so no excuses.

So-called writer's block is simply FEAR, but when you sit down and concentrate and focus on the story at hand, you erase that fear. Writing is a habit. Develop that habit and you keep the big, bad "blocks" away.

HAVE IT FOR ME YESTERDAY

While we're on the subject of bugaboos, here's another one—DEAD-LINES. They're a major part of any writing experience. Deadlines are something you'll find in all businesses, except for the guys who remodel your kitchen.

As a working TV comedy writer, you will always be expected to work a lot more quickly than you had planned to, and that means you can't wait until you "feel like it." Picture yourself as a homeless person, rotting away in a nameless gutter. Works for me.

YARN-SPINNING 101

Congratulations! Boot camp is over. Now your story will begin to breathe as you write an actual FIRST DRAFT. You are about to create a new reality. A "life" that never existed before. Egad! It's Frankenscript!

You will weave your ideas into action and put words into the actors' mouths. And although it's true that many actors refuse to acknowledge the existence of writers, and prefer to promote the fantasy that they make up the lines as they go along, the fact is that they should be kneeling down and sucking our literary toes for making them appear human.

But I digress . . . I wasn't talking about sucking toes, I was talking about the First Draft, which is a play (teleplay) told in TWO ACTS. It is a story told with pictures, and supported by mirth-provoking dialogue. It's my favorite part of the writing process. Why, you ask? Well, I consider myself a playwright, and now's my chance to create a wonderful play to be performed.

THAT PROFESSIONAL LOOK

It's time to address the TV sitcom FORMAT—the way a TV script should look, in a form that's pretty much the standard. The entire thirty-minute teleplay is in Two Acts, totaling around fifty pages (although your First Draft can go a little longer), but try to keep the script you submit to a manageable fifty to fifty-five pages. Remember that you are filling twenty-four minutes of scintillating air time, the remaining six minutes (and growing) devoted to commercials and promos for other shows during the credits (which are crammed into a small box in the corner of your screen so no one will bother trying to read them).

So what does a script look like? Well, the best way to familiarize yourself with the format is to obtain a copy of a real sitcom script, preferably a script from the show you are writing for. That's what I did when I started writing my "spec" script, and seeing the real script form erased a lot of the fears I had. TV and movie scripts can be obtained from SCRIPT CITY in Hollywood, CA. Call for a free catalogue at (323) 871-0707. For orders only, you can call toll-free at (800) 676-2522.

To give you an good idea of what a script looks like, here's a scene from an unsold pilot script of mine called *Paradise Shores*—an anthology about people who meet at an Hawaiian vacation resort:

<u>ACT ONE</u>

<u>SCENE A</u>

<u>FADE IN:</u>

<u>INT. CONDO - BATHROOM - DAY</u>

WE HEAR A <u>MAN'S VOICE</u> SINGING IN THE SHOWER.

                         GUY

           Washin' that gal outta my hair—
           La-dee-do, and I-I-I-I don't care . . . !

<u>SFX: PERSISTENT DOORBELL.</u>

THE VOICE STOPS SINGING.

INT. CONDO - LIVING ROOM - CONTINUOUS

GUY ASHER, A MAN IN HIS LATE 30s, BURSTS OUT OF THE
BATHROOM, DRIPPING WET IN A BATHROBE. HE OPENS THE DOOR, AND
IN POPS A WOMAN'S HAND, ITS FINGERS FLAPPING UP AND DOWN
LIKE A PUPPET.

> HAROLD HAND
>
> (SHRILL PUPPET VOICE) Hi! I'm
> your next door neighbor, Harold
> Hand! You have great eyes!

A PAUSE—GUY DOESN'T KNOW HOW TO REACT TO THIS. THE HAND
BEGINS TO SHAKE.

> HAROLD HAND (CONT'D)
>
> Okay, I seem to be bombing, so
> heeeere goes . . . (AN ENTHUSIASTIC
> INTRO) . . . Gentleman and gentleman—
> Selma Feewig!!

SELMA FEEWIG HESITANTLY APPEARS IN THE DOORWAY. SHE'S IN HER
EARLY 30s, CUTE, BUT NOT WHAT YOU WOULD CALL A
KNOCKOUT.

> SELMA
>
> Hello . . .

SELMA FUMBLES IN HER LARGE, BOTTOMLESS POCKETBOOK, COMES UP
WITH A CAKE, AND PUSHES THE PAN AT HIM.

> SELMA (CONT'D)
>
> . . . I made coffee cake. Some
> of the top is still in my bag,
> but the real flavor is in
> the middle.

> GUY

(STUNNED) Who are you?

> SELMA

Your neighbor . . . and since we're
neighbors, I thought we might
sit and be neighborly.

> GUY

(BEWILDERED) What? . . . Oh, right,
sure . . . c'mon in . . .

> HAROLD HAND

(TO SELMA) I think he's trying to
hit on you.

GUY DOES A SURPRISED TAKE AT HAROLD.

> SELMA

(TO HER HAND) Harold, you shush now!

HAROLD IS QUICKLY WHIPPED AWAY.

> GUY

(STUDIES HER, THEN) Your lips
— they move.

> SELMA

I beg your pardon?

> GUY

When you're Harold, your lips
move.

> SELMA

Well, Harold isn't a puppet,
Harold's a hand.

                         GUY

Even so, I have a sneaking
suspicion that what your hand
is saying, is coming from you.

                         SELMA

Well, yes . . . I suppose it is . . .
(THEN) Actually, my hand is an
experiment. You may not believe
this, but I used to be shy as
a bat.

                         GUY

It's blind as a bat.

                         SELMA

I see fine.

                         GUY

No, bats are blind.

                         SELMA

Then what are shy?

                         GUY

(IMPATIENTLY) What's the difference?!

                         SELMA

Lots of things. My hand helped
me conquer my shyness. First,
I tried taking uppers, but I
wrecked my car. Then, lucky for
me, my analyst, Dr. Callahan,
suggested my hand. It worked
for him. In fact, he's gone from
talking through his hand to a
little dummy he calls Danny O'Freud.

GUY JUST STARES. SELMA IS ROLLING AND ANXIOUS TO KEEP THIS
EXPERIENCE ALIVE.

                         SELMA (CONT'D)

    I saw you in the restaurant last
    night. We were three tables from
    each other, gagging on the same poi.

                         GUY

    I'd rather eat glue.

                         SELMA

    How'cum your wife wasn't eating
    glue with you?

                         GUY

    I don't have a wife. I'm divorced.

                         SELMA

    Ohhhhhhhh . . . this must be a trying
    time for you. I'm soooo sorry.

                         GUY

    Save yourself the trouble.

                         SELMA

    You poor man . . .

                         GUY

    I'm not poor . . .

                         SELMA

    That poor woman.

                    GUY

Just whose side are you on anyway?
(REALIZES THE INANITY OF THIS
CONVERSATION) Look, don't be on
anybody's side. There are no sides.
I mean, she all of a sudden tells
me that she doesn't love me anymore
. . . She tells me she's fallen for
her ceramics teacher—their hands
met on his spinner . . . Why am I
telling you this?

                    SELMA

Because you need somebody to talk
to.

                    GUY

Yeah, well, I did everything that
was expected of a husband . . . I was
faithful to that woman for sixteen
years and she left me! But I'm not
gonna lie down and die—I'm going
right out there to grab myself a
future!

                    SELMA

What a coincidence, I'm single
and here to grab myself a future
too. I'm finding my way through
'BEEMEE.'

                    GUY

What's a Beemee?

                    SELMA

B-e-e-m-e-e—it stands for
                    (MORE)

                         SELMA (CONT'D)

          'b-e m-e'—it's a seminar
          devoted to individuality.
          Today's topic is on finding
          out who you really are.

                              GUY

          Well, I hope you find out.

                            SELMA

          Not likely, the seminar's already
          started—but that's okay, I can
          always find myself tomorrow . . . So,
          are you gonna be here long?

                              GUY

          Seven glorious, fun-filled days.

                            SELMA

          Me too! Isn't it grand? The two
          of us, here on vacation—free
          not to be ourselves.

                              GUY

          (SMILES) It's nice to meet you
          neighbor.

                            SELMA

          Believe me, it's fate.

A PAUSE. SELMA TRIES TO KEEP THINGS MOVING ALONG.

                         SELMA (CONT'D)

          Do you ever see women, like,
          y'know, as friends . . . ?

                    GUY

I don't have any friends. They
picked between me and my wife
. . . I think she bribed them.

                    SELMA

. . . Do you think WE could be friends?
(PLOWS AHEAD) I mean, don't let the
fact that I have webbed feet throw
you . . .

                    GUY

(PUZZLED) You have webbed feet?

                    SELMA

Of course not, don't be silly.

                    GUY

Have you noticed that not once
since you came in have you
talked through your hand?

                    SELMA

Yeah, I noticed.

                    GUY

Hey, friend, how about a walk on the
beach?

                    SELMA

(BEAMS) Sure!

SELMA'S HAND SHOOTS UP.

```
                    HAROLD HAND

           (TO GUY) She promises not to lay a
           hand on you . . . but I should warn you
           that she is a tiger when provoked.
                                           CUT TO:
```

NITTY AND GRITTY

Okay, now that you've had a chance to see a script sample, the following FORMAT REQUIREMENTS should be pointed out:

1. The scenes are always identified. <u>ACT ONE, SCENE A</u>, <u>ACT ONE, SCENE B</u>, and so on. Some shows use scene numbers instead of letters. All are <u>underlined</u>.
2. All tape and film scripts begin with the words <u>FADE IN:</u> (<u>underlined</u>). The final scenes in Act One and Act Two always end with the words <u>FADE OUT.</u> Act Two opens with <u>FADE IN:</u> again.
3. Each scene begins by describing where we are: <u>INT.</u> <u>CONDO - BATHROOM - DAY.</u> <u>INT.</u> for "Interior." <u>EXT.</u> for "Exterior." <u>CONTINUOUS</u> if the scene is an uninterrupted flow from the previous scene. All are <u>underlined</u>.
4. You then double-space to a brief narrative line: WE HEAR A MAN'S VOICE SINGING IN THE SHOWER. Narrative lines are in CAPS, and if there is more than one line it is single-spaced.

<u>NOTE:</u> Formats may vary slightly for individual sitcoms. If you refer back to the sample *Welcome Back, Kotter* scene, you will see that the narrative is in parentheses. This is the way *Kotter* scripts were written. In the previous example, I didn't use parentheses. This is no big deal—parentheses are optional—but if you have a script sample of the show you are writing, follow it religiously.

5. The margin for the character's name is mid-page. Roughly fifty single spaces from the left margin.
6. The dialogue margin is approximately thirty-five single spaces from the left margin. These character and dialogue

spaces vary slightly with every show. That's why it's
great if you can get a sample script of the show you are
writing to eyeball and use as your guide.

7. All dialogue is double-spaced.

8. If a character's dialogue continues onto the next page, it
is formatted in this way:

```
                    GUY

    . . . She tells me she's fallen for
    her ceramics teacher—their hands
                  (MORE)
```

(new page)
```
               GUY (CONT'D)

    met on his spinner . . . Why am I
    telling you this?
```

9. Any actor's direction (STUNNED) (BEWILDERED) (TO
SELMA) are capitalized and in parentheses.

10. All scenes end with CUT TO: to describe a transition to
the next scene. (Use CAPS and underline). If the scene is
CONTINUOUS, there is no CUT TO:.

11. When moving to a NEW SCENE, never continue on the
same page. Move to the next page.

12. Don't number your scenes. This is a format device generally associated with the screenplay form.

13. At the end of Act One (after FADE OUT), write END OF
ACT ONE (CAPS and underline.) Repeat this process for
Act Two.

14. A reminder about TEASERS and TAGS—those pesky little scenes that get us in or out of the show. DON'T be
concerned about these when writing your "spec" script.
Your job is to tell a good, solid story in Two Acts.

15. P-l-e-a-s-e NUMBER your pages! Once, a writer gave me a
screenplay to read, and had neglected to number the pages,
or to even fasten them together. I accidentally dropped the
pages on the floor, where they remain to this very day.

16. And, finally, notice the absence of Camera Angles. Don't bother with these. No matter how avant-garde they may be, they are not generally used in sitcom. The director is king of the camera, and he will only scratch your angles out. All directors hate it when writers try to do their job for them. Let the director direct. He may do a stinko job, but that's the way the system works.

That being said, it's time for me to haul out another disclaimer, so I don't appear to be a liar. I have to admit that in the "I Am the King" revised story outline, I used some camera angles in the scene where Dennis is at home, watching Charlie on TV:

SHOT - DENNIS

BACK TO TV SCREEN

Well, I had to. The scene demanded that I indicate the pictures I wanted the audience to see. Instances like this are rare in sitcom, and I still don't encourage the use of camera angles. Your job is to write the script, not direct it.

Once you see an actual script and get a feel for how it really looks, a lot of the fear goes away. You've cleared another hurdle, and it's no longer all that mysterious. In fact, you are now prepared to "go to script" and write your First Draft.

WORDS ON PAPER

Your initial stab at a First Draft will likely be long and overwritten and that's the way it should be. You've got to be flexible. Go where the scenes take you and you may happily find yourself in places where you never expected to be. I love when that happens.

Stick to your story outline as much as possible, but remember that this is a work in progress, so don't be afraid to veer off into the unknown and EXPERIMENT. You can always go back and cut what you don't need. Sometimes you have to get from (A) to (C) by writing (B). Then you suddenly discover that you don't need (B)—and without (B), (A) and (C) blend together very nicely, thank you.

This happens all the time. For example, Shakespeare wrote (A) "To be or not to be." He followed it with (B) "You know what I'm sayin'?" And he finished with (C) "That is the question." When reviewing his work, Shakespeare decided that the phrase worked better by cutting (B). But he never would have been able to link (A) and (C) without having written (B). And that's a fact.

Writing a First Draft is a lot like farming. You continually fertilize and plow your way ahead. Plant words on paper. Feel free to be silly! Dare yourself to sound stupid! No one, except you, is seeing this, and you can always cut what doesn't work as you go along.

Don't worry over JOKES. We'll tackle those little guys later. If a funny line comes to you, by all means preserve it. But if you're stuck for high humor, don't sweat it: Come back to it later. I always write "JTC" (Joke To Come) in the margin when I'm temporarily stuck for wit.

Your main goal—as you take this first plunge through your script—is to TELL THE STORY. The jokes will follow.

A First Draft is an organic, continually changing method of development. It's creative expression, and very much a CRAFT. As writers, we are all in the rug-weaving business, the only difference being that our rugs can get up and talk.

NARRATIVE

Narrative refers to those descriptive lines that precede or intersect dialogue. An example of narrative in the *Paradise Shores* script reads: WE HEAR A MAN'S VOICE SINGING IN THE SHOWER. The next narrative line is SFX: PERSISTENT DOORBELL.

SFX is writer code for Sound Effect. The third narrative line is THE VOICE STOPS SINGING. In the narrative that follows, the character is simply described as GUY ASHER, A MAN IN HIS LATE 30s, DRIPPING WET IN A BATHROBE. This is minimal, economical, no frills writing.

In a feature film, a screenwriter may write:

VESTIGES OF DAY GONE TO DUSK CAST LONG SLIVERS OF LIGHT ON A STEAMY SHOWER DOOR. WE HEAR THE STRAINS

OF A HAPPY, YET DISSONANT TUNE IN A VOICE RIDDLED
WITH DOUBT AND DEPRESSION. THE SONG IS CUT SHORT BY
THE INSISTENT RING, RING, RINGING OF A TIRED DOORBELL
IN NEED OF REPAIR. A WET SHADOW THAT IS GUY ASHER
EMERGES FROM THE SHOWER, HIS TIRED EYES CONVEYING A
LOOK OF ONE SEXUALLY DISPOSSESSED

. . . and so on and so on and crapola.

Avoid this sort of driveling on in a teleplay. I don't even recommend it for a screenplay. Nobody gives a rat's petootie how good
you are at writing prose. No one cares that you once wrote a fifty-
page essay on nose hair that won you a prize. This is not a novel you
are writing here. Just write down the facts of the situation—quickly,
succinctly, to the point.

The next chunk of narrative is: HE OPENS THE DOOR,
AND IN POPS A <u>WOMAN'S HAND</u>, ITS FINGERS FLAPPING UP
AND DOWN LIKE A PUPPET. This describes the action as briefly as
possible. If a specific piece of action or a prop is important, then you
must write it in.

For example, if it's essential to the story that Cosmo Kramer
is dancing on the counter, dressed as a radish, let us know about it,
but be brief. Tell the person reading the script only what she NEEDS
TO KNOW. It moves the process along quickly, and enhances your
chances for success.

ARCHIE BUNKER LIVES!

Some pages back, I told you that a sitcom plot is driven by the character(s) and that engaging story-telling depends on the human element. If you don't remember me talking about this, go back and read it again, because in sitcom (and all fiction writing) CHARACTER IS EVERYTHING!

Okay, you're in the process of writing your First Draft. You have developed an educated approach to the task by gaining a swift knowledge of Format and Narrative. Now it's time for you to take a good look at DEVELOPING CHARACTER and DIALOGUE.

A good writer is a people-watcher—an astute observer of human behavior. Screenwriters and novelists create characters through imagination and experience. But TV comedy offers the writer an advantage—the characters have already been created through the original writer's imagination and experience. These characters have faces, voices, preconceived ideas about the world they inhabit every week.

Sitcom characters have a POINT OF VIEW. How they view the world or the situation they find themselves in reveals who they are. All sitcom characters have an ATTITUDE about life, and that attitude guides their behavior and what they say.

An excellent example of POINT OF VIEW and an ATTITUDE that reveals character is brilliantly illustrated in an episode of *Home Improvement,* where the issue under discussion is the family dishwasher.

Tim doesn't see why he has to rinse the dishes before putting them in the dishwasher. Jill tells him the spray's not strong enough. Tim snarls at her for not getting a "man's" dishwasher and offers to fix the spray. Jill begs him not to get out his tools and play because, every time he fixes something, something gets unfixed. Tim tenaciously pursues the issue; Jill continues to resist.

This scene is loaded with ATTITUDE and tells us an awful lot about the well-defined characters of Tim and Jill. In fact, the whole *Home Improvement* series depicted a very real relationship between two, strong-willed married people with opposing views on many things.

Getting back to *Seinfeld,* we can confidently predict that the characters, being a competitive bunch, will try their best to win "The Contest." When Jerry predicts that Kramer won't last beyond the paying of the check, he's being utterly realistic. Jerry knows Kramer. Sure enough, Kramer is the first one to lose the bet. How this happens (the naked lady seen through the window) is amusing storytelling, and oh-so-true to the character of Kramer.

The characters in *Seinfeld* all have a NEED in "The Contest"—something they wish to accomplish—which is winning. What each one does to achieve that goal shows us character. And if it reveals a character trait we haven't seen before, well, that's terrific writing. Showing a character in the process of GROWTH always makes for an excellent teleplay.

Laughs are the beating heart of comedy TV, and when a character says something the writer thinks is funny, the humor should never be put INTO the character, it should come OUT of the character. It's that character expressing her own, unique, somewhat offbeat point of view. Note this fine example from the "Dharma's Tangled Web" episode of *Dharma & Greg,* written by Bill Prady and Regina Stewart:

<u>DHARMA APPEARS OUTSIDE THE WINDOW BY THE PIANO</u>, HOLDING A
PASTA MAKER. SHE TAPS ON THE GLASS TO GET KITTY'S ATTENTION.

                         DHARMA

            Ding dong! Mammogram!

                          KITTY

            (STARTLED) What?

                         DHARMA

            It just sounds like something that
            should be delivered, doesn't it?

<u>DHARMA CROSSES OUT</u>. KITTY CROSSES TO MAKE HERSELF A DRINK.

                          KITTY

            (CALMING HERSELF) And it's our
            daughter-in-law, and we're pleasant,
            and we're talking to ourselves.

<u>DHARMA ENTERS</u>.

                         DHARMA

            Brought you back your pasta maker.

                          KITTY

            Ah, thank you, Dharma.

                         DHARMA

            You didn't know I borrowed it, did you?

                          KITTY

            No, no, I didn't.

                         DHARMA

            Didn't know you had one, did you?

KITTY

Well, you got me again.

DHARMA

You thought a pasta maker was a
person, didn't you?

KITTY

Please, stop.

DHARMA LOOKS AROUND THE ROOM AND GASPS.

DHARMA

Oh my God —

KITTY

What?

DHARMA

You and Edward split up.

KITTY

Why on earth would you say that?

DHARMA

Well, it's obvious. Look at
Edward's favorite chair, there's no
butt indentation. And look here,
Edward's pipe (SNUFFING IT) hasn't
been smoked for at least three days.
And here in the paper—no one's
solved the Jumble.

KITTY

Fascinating, Sherlock, however this
is a new chair; it arrived this
morning. The pipe is not Edward's,
                (MORE)

> KITTY (CONT'D)
>
> it's Thomas Jefferson's. We bought
> it at auction, it hasn't been smoked
> in two hundred years. As for the
> Jumble, Edward never solves it. He
> just laughs at the little cartoon.
>
> DHARMA
>
> Wow, I'm not usually wrong about
> these things.

EDWARD CROSSES PAST IN THE HALLWAY, CARRYING A GARMENT
BAG. HE DOESN'T SEE DHARMA.

> EDWARD
>
> This is the last of my shirts. If
> you need anything, I'll be at my
> apartment.
>
> DHARMA
>
> (TO KITTY) Thomas Jefferson.

In only a few pages, the writers have provided us with a pretty clear idea of who Dharma is—as well as some good insights into the characters of her in-laws, Kitty and Edward.

Too many sitcoms today sacrifice humor drawn from character for crude attempts at being funny. How many times have you seen two sitcom characters swapping semifunny quips just for the sake of swapping semifunny quips? Or kids saying things a kid would never say, just so the writer can attempt to appear witty? Not with *Dharma & Greg*. This is a true character comedy.

The best humor comes from ATTITUDE, PERSONALITY, BEHAVIOR—all adding up to form CHARACTER. CHARACTER IS REVELATION. We learn about people by what they do and how they express themselves. These examples from a *Spin City* episode, titled "The Goodbye Girl" by Gayle Abrams, tell us a lot about the characters of Michael and the Mayor:

MICHAEL AND THE MAYOR ARE THERE. THE MAYOR IS AT
THE WINDOW.

                    MAYOR

What a beautiful woman.

                    MICHAEL

The Statue of Liberty, sir?

                    MAYOR

Jennifer.

                    MICHAEL

Damn.

                    MAYOR

It's been twenty-nine years since
I've had a first kiss. What were
you doing twenty-nine years ago,
Mike?

                    MICHAEL

Breast feeding. And I think we
should move on.

                    MAYOR

I tell you, I feel like I'm
walking on air. (THEN) You'll
have to forgive my exuberance,
Mike, but it's not easy meeting
women when you're the Mayor. It's
not like I could go where any
normal guy would go to meet
girls: pottery class, produce
section, Vietnam War rally.

                    MICHAEL

Those are the big three. Listen,
                    (MORE)

MICHAEL (CONT'D)

I'm happy for you, sir, really I
am. But when the public sees a
recently divorced man running
around with a woman who is, oh,
for the sake of argument, let's
say, younger than him, it might
seem inappropriate. In fact, some
people might even think you were
seeing her while you were married.

MAYOR

I wish.

MICHAEL

Sir, it's very difficult to get re-
elected on the "I wish I cheated"
platform.

MAYOR

Well, I suppose I could be
discreet for a little while.

MICHAEL

That would be great, sir.

MAYOR

How long are we talking?

MICHAEL

Just a few months.

MAYOR

How many?

MICHAEL

Sixty.

(Later, in the episode, when the Mayor's relationship doesn't work out.)

                        MAYOR

          They're closing the last
          Woolworth's in the city. Twenty
          years ago, women flocked to that
          store, Mike. Now they don't think
          it's flashy enough. It's too old-
          fashioned. It's obsolete.

                        MICHAEL

          Sir, I drove by there last week.
          There were still quite a lot of
          ladies clamoring to get in.

                        MAYOR

          Blue hairs, Mike. They're there
          to buy yarn.

                        MICHAEL

          You're wrong. People love Woolworth's
          because it's a classic, and quality
          never goes out of style. As far as I'm
          concerned, any woman who can't see
          that shouldn't be allowed in the store.

                        MAYOR

          Yeah, but that store was married
          to one . . . customer for twenty-five
          years and this new customer is the
          first shopper to . . . Ah, the hell
          with it, I'm talking about me,
          Mike.

                        MICHAEL

          I figured it, sir. That's why you're
          the undisputed king of the
          metaphor.

MAYOR

Don't try to cheer me up. I'm a
crumbling brick building. I was
too old for her.

MICHAEL

You are not too old. You're mature.
And women want mature. Do you
know how many women have told me
to call them when I mature?

In just these few short scenes, the writer has managed to reveal quite a lot about Michael and the Mayor. It's done with wit and economy— and that's good "character" writing.

YADA-YADA-YADA

WORDS are the writer's connection with an audience. We take words from our minds and simply place them in the character's mouths. We do this through DIALOGUE—words that are written for actors, words that are meant to be spoken.

My experience as an actor has helped me a lot when I write dialogue. I am able to "be" the character, and hear the character "speak" to me. This kind of mental defect is a real plus for any writer.

One special thing about dialogue—especially comic dialogue—is that you get to "play with the language" in colorful ways. You get to ask yourself questions like:

"If lawyers are disbarred and clergymen defrocked, does it follow that electricians can be delighted, cowboys deranged, dogs debarked, and cleaners depressed?" It's an old joke, but one that poses penetrating questions. Think about them.

Dialogue ILLUMINATES. It constantly reveals something about the characters' Point of View and who they are. The words should sound natural. A good writer has an "ear" for the many varieties of actual human speech. Americans do not speak in unclouded prose. We skip words, talk in half-sentences, sometimes we don't even complete our thoughts. We use CONTRACTIONS and SLANG. Got to is "gotta." Want to is "wanna." Ought to is "oughta."

Check out this excerpt from *Kotter*'s "Whodunit?" Horshack thinks Rosalie "Hotsie" Totsie really is pregnant and he wants to do the right thing. Listen to the language.

(<u>ROSALIE APPEARS</u> AND ALL THE SWEATHOGS
SPLIT—EXCEPT FOR HORSHACK.)

                    HORSHACK

Rosalie, can I talk to ya for a minute?

                    ROSALIE

Sure, Arnold, shoot.

                    HORSHACK

Rosalie—are ya doin' anything on
Saturday?

                    ROSALIE

Why?

                    HORSHACK

Ya wanna get married?

                    ROSALIE

Why would I wanna do that?

                    HORSHACK

'Cause I like ya—and wanna make
ya honest and give yer baby a name.
Y'know, Horshack's an old and
respected name. It's Polish . . . It means
"the cattle are dying."

                    ROSALIE

It's really sweet of you to offer, Arnold,
but I wanna marry the father of my
baby—and you couldn't be the father.

HORSHACK

Why not?

ROSALIE

Arnold, dont'cha remember? Nothin'
ever happened.

HORSHACK

Oh, yeah . . . Well, think about it, Rosalie.
I mean, at least if you married me, you
wouldn't be Hotsie Totsie no more.

(HORSHACK EXITS. ROSALIE LOOKS OFF, THINKS.)

ROSALIE

(TO HERSELF) Great, I'd be Hotsie
Horshack.

See how dialogue illuminates character? Horshack and Rosalie come
from a tough area of Brooklyn, and this is reflected in their dialogue.

Never forget that a good writer is a good LISTENER, familiar
with realistic patterns of the way people talk.

There is a catch, though. Dialogue can't be TOO real because
actual human conversation can be pretty boring, and we must always
remember that we are writing to ENTERTAIN. Hence, there is a popular use of "Fake Realism" in TV comedy. Characters are required to
express themselves in a funny way. If they don't, they'll soon be off
the air and the actors will be back selling Amway.

Guess what, though? Yup, there's another catch. A sitcom
doesn't HAVE to be joke-filled for absolutely every moment. It's okay
to let dialogue take an occasional serious turn. If a situation is serious,
don't be afraid to BE serious in your intent. Play out the emotional
reality. *Sports Night* is not afraid to be serious—a sometimes-serious
tone adds quality to the show's stories, and heightens the comedy.

Viewers enjoy warm, genuine moments between sitcom
characters. People like having their feelings tugged at a little. Then,

when the writer skillfully follows the serious with a joke or some physical schtick, it eases the audience's mood, breaks the tension, gets a laugh before turning back into comedy mode. Being serious is never a problem for a humorist—we're all sad clowns underneath.

When Horshack proposed to Rosalie in the previous scene, it was serious in intent, but liberally laced with jokes. For the very finest example of combining funny with serious, take a look at any episode of *M*A*S*H.*

YADA-YADA-YADA (CONT'D)

When writing dialogue, take into account the ACTING STYLES of the actors you are writing for. Pay attention to the way they sound, the RHYTHMS of their speech. The lines you write should reflect the actor as well as the character the actor is portraying. Actors inhabit their characters on a weekly basis, and they know the character a lot better than any dweeb writer! At least that's what a lot of dweeb actors have told me. So beware! Writing dialogue that changes an actor's take on the character is a sure-fire way to cultivate resentment and dirty looks.

Dialogue should be approached as "experimental." Trial and error. Don't be afraid to write bad lines at first—just get the basic idea on paper. If it's not funny right away, don't worry, you can always go back and funny it up later.

SCHMENDRICK'S FUNNIER THAN JERK

Certain WORDS are funnier than others. The sounds of some words will generate laughter where others won't.

Words with a "k" sound always score big. Cupcake, creep, kangaroo, ke-bob, kibitz, kinky, klutz, kazoo, you get the idea. In comedy writing, a dog is never just a dog; it is a Spitz or, better yet Schnauzer. Funny sounds.

If a person is annoying, he is never referred to as just a person; he is a schmoid or a dipstick or whatever else strikes you as funny. Pickle is funny, tickle is funny—all the "-ickle" words are funny.

Hard sounds always score, too. Many of them derive from the original Yiddish—words like putz, yutz, and schmutz. Isn't this fun?

There are NAMES that are funnier than others, too. Shirley, Herbie, and Mimsy are funnier (have a funnier sound) than Peter, Paul, or Mary. Here's an example:

A grasshopper walks into a bar and orders a drink. "My God," says the bartender, "a talking grasshopper! We have a drink named after you!" The grasshopper looks at the bartender in amazement and says, "IRVING"?

"Irving" is a funny name. All guys named Irving know this. Women marry guys named Irving so they'll always have something to laugh at. If I had ended the joke with the name "Kevin" or "Matt," the sound isn't right and I would have diminished my response . . . if there was any.

Certain names of CITIES are funnier than others. Oshkosh, Sheboygan, and Cucamonga are funnier than Portland, Racine, or Springfield.

The same goes for the names of FOODS. Weiner, Tutti-Frutti, and Kumquat are funnier than Apple, Steak, or Lettuce.

Let's take BRAND NAMES. Tidy-Bowl, Ding-Dongs, and Snausages will get much bigger guffaws than Papermate, Carnation, or Canada Dry. Screaming Yellow Zonkers are in a class all their own.

Playing with words—funny words—is a game I indulge in all the time. You should play it too. It's fun, and will add a whole lotta ammo to your comedy writing arsenal.

FILTH IN DIALOGUE

Many young comics today feel that they have to be dirty to be funny, and it's funny how good they are at being dirty. All they have to do now is work harder at being funny.

When I was working the sitcom-go-round, the writing staff would always get a report on the script which had been read by the network's "Standards & Practices" department (CENSORS for short). These censors were a strange lot—you have to be when your only job is to look for smut. Their script reports were always great fun to read, and when cut at just the right angles, made excellent snowflakes. These censors were obsessed with their mission. They were here on loan from God to clean up the world and keep it safe for sponsors, and they would constantly find offensive material where none was intended.

I recall one ABC censor (a former Las Vegas showgirl) who was having difficulty finding offensive material in the *Welcome Back, Kotter* scripts, so she picked at any little thing that looked suspicious. For instance, once, one of the writers used the word "bat"—as in baseball bat—but she saw it as a phallic reference, and the offensive word had to be removed. Anyhow, it got to the point where my fellow writers and I decided to purposely put questionable things in the scripts in order for her to justify her job. She was delighted, and it got her a promotion.

Today, the job of the censors is being taken over by a movement that is out to rob us of our individuality, to wash all of our minds and hang them on a straight party line. That movement is called "Political Correctness." (Now, there are two words without a single thought.) Political correctness is antihumor. Avoid falling into its trap at all costs. I mean, when you think about it, what's correct about politics?

COMEDY ALERT!

I don't believe in censorship in any form. I do believe in being responsible for the kinds of stuff you put out on national TV. Today, humorous dialogue is being downsized. Sexual innuendo is considered high humor. Grossness is being mistaken for wit. Crude is cool. Wee-wee jokes are the most popular way of getting a laugh. Except for a very few, fine exceptions, too much of today's sitcom dialogue is geared to reach the lowest common denominator—the stupid level. We've gone from fun and funnier to dumb and dumber.

Today's TV executives are developing a generation of children whose senses of humor are not being nurtured—they're being STARVED. These poor kids are being forced to settle for less, and they don't even know it. As a result, we're on our way to becoming a less funny, more serious public—a public in which comedy is dim and violence is easier to accept. Yeah . . . mull that over for awhile.

I feel that the only way to remedy this dismal situation is to send the TV industry a message, and that message is, "I'm mad as hell, and I'm not WATCHING anymore!" That'll make the bureaucratic fur fly.

A Second Opinion

Party time! Put on that stupid jester hat and celebrate! On your hot little desk you have an entire First Draft script out of your very own head. Compare your script to the sample you've been using. Make sure it's the right length and in the proper format. A script that's overlong or ignores the rules of format is a sure sign of amateurism, which is punishable by being either ignored or rejected or both. If, however, all seems well, good, and funny, grasp that sucker in both hands, raise it high above your head and say something terribly funny. Like what? Hey, you're a comedy writer now. You'll think of something.

There's a great sense of accomplishment at this stage of the sitcom writing process, and you have every reason to feel proud of yourself. In your hands, you hold your future—<u>FADE IN</u> to <u>FADE OUT</u>—and nothing but gold in between. Well, maybe not exactly gold. There might be some dirt and a few rocks mixed in. Perhaps it's time to take another look at your script? After all, nobody gets it all right the first time. The last person to do that was crucified.

What you have here is a "rough" draft. Words on paper. You've worked out the script as best as you could, but is it really there yet? Could it be funnier? Are there any story or character glitches? Are there things that you have hidden doubts about, that you're not quite sure of? Don't hope that people won't notice because they most certainly will, so take off that stupid jester hat and get back to work on a SECOND DRAFT.

The Second Draft is a REWRITE of the First Draft. (As if you didn't know.) Personally, I think this is where the "real" writing begins. I love the process of adding, refining, shaping, editing, polishing, crafting. Separating the Krispies from the Rice. If Charles Dickens hadn't believed in rewriting, the opening line of A CHRISTMAS CAROL could very well have read: "Marley was alive . . . " And Marley has to be dead or there's no ghost story. Without rewriting, the opening line of Herman Melville's MOBY DICK would be "Call me Herbie" . . . and you might not be so compelled to keep reading.

Oscar Wilde showed his own, unique take on rewriting when he said: "All morning I worked on the draft of one of my poems, and I took out a comma. In the afternoon, I put it back."

Unfortunately, we don't all achieve perfection on the first try as Oscar Wilde did, so take another close look at your script. Follow your hunches. If a joke doesn't sound quite right to you, don't avoid it. Confront it, look it straight in the punchline, and rework it. Then dump it if necessary. If your story has a crack in it, set to work repairing that crack, before it sucks you in and you're never heard from again.

The really neat thing about writing is that you get a second chance at correcting what you didn't get right the first time. You are constantly challenged to "top" yourself and, by topping yourself, you create a more inventive reality. Keep in mind that issues of pride and ego have no place here. In the writing game, the work is all, the play's the thing. Blow your own horn after you win the Emmy.

THE LITERARY HAIRCUT

Great writing is great EDITING. If a piece of dialogue or an entire scene doesn't seem to be working, examine the possibility of CUTTING—peeling away the excess. What you want is likely there, the marble just needs to be chipped away. If you can remove a line, a block of dialogue, or even an entire scene in your script and not miss it, you never needed it. So CUT IT! It's slowing down the pace of your story.

KNOW WHEN TO FOLD 'EM

Comedy writers have a habit of falling in love with their material. Especially jokes. The idea of cutting any object of love is akin to blowing your nose in the holy grail. I have a file drawer filled with jokes that I loved, but had to finally cut because they were disturbing the flow. I vowed that I would use these jokes again someday, and I never have. As you go through this revisionary rewriting process, watch out for overkill, overconcern, self-doubt. If your script suddenly doesn't seem as funny or make as much sense, this could be a danger sign—a sign that it's time to stop. A superabundance of attention can utterly destroy a scene or a joke you improvised off the top of your head. When a writer gets obsessive about changes, craftsmanship can turn into crapsmanship. So watch carefully that you don't reject some of your initial hunches—things that are on the money. Too much feeding has killed many a goldfish. Know when it's time to "let go" and allow your script to leave the nest.

DO YOU LIKE IT? DO YOU REALLY LIKE IT?

The completion of your rewrite means that judgment day is here! You're going to want someone to read what you have written. You are about to place your "baby" in the hands of another, so PLEASE be sure those hands belong to someone whose opinion you trust. Someone with a good sense of humor. If that person loves what you've written, put that stupid jester hat back on and make whoopee! If that person has "problems" with what you have written, cool the whoopee, listen patiently to what that person has to say, then decide for yourself what you think he or she might be right about. After all, you're the boss, you wrote this little gem, and the final decisions are yours. Whatever you do, don't take a defensive stance. Be open to new (and maybe better) ideas. A healthy dose of objectivity can go far toward improving a script.

But if the person whose opinion you trust tells you your script stinks, you face a problem. Also a day that is not going at all well. What to do? Well, don't overreact, just find a NEW person whose opinion you trust.

Above all, never cave in to criticism. Avoid compromising your initial, good hunches. Stick with those hunches because they're right.

And when you finally have a finished product, present it to the world with CONFIDENCE. Be optimistic. Sure-minded. Never think in terms of failure. I recall this friend of mine. For years he thought he was a failure, but I told him to be positive. Now he's positive he's a failure.

GIGGLES, GOOFS, AND GUFFAWS

You know what I really cherish about comedy writing? JOKES! They're blatantly politically INcorrect—illogically logical—and a wonderfully effective way of pointing out the absurdities in life. They project ordinary ideas extraordinarily by seeing and saying things in ways no one else has seen or said them before. Best of all, they're a great exercise in playing with our very colorful language.

Successful television comedy is based on two important questions:

"WHAT WOULD THE CHARACTER THINK IN THIS SITUATION?"

"HOW WOULD THE CHARACTER EXPRESS THAT THOUGHT?"

These questions allow you to think abstractly—to seize a golden opportunity to lay in a zinger. A savvy TV comedy writer never passes up the chance for a joke. Jokes are the LIFEBLOOD of a sitcom script, so it's essential that I devote plenty of time to this subject. Here goes—

A joke has been defined as a VERBAL DECEPTION—a trick played on your mind. Your thoughts are led in one direction, then a rug is pulled out from under your head. Your job as a comedy writer is to pull out that rug. Control the audience's thoughts. Get them to picture some "image" in their minds (the SET-UP), and then sock them with the unexpected at the end (the PUNCHLINE). The Set-Up (or straight line) "sets up" an expectation. The Punchline "derails" that expectation with a punch. The writer outwits the audience and they laugh in surprise.

Here's an example from Garry Shandling. Is it what you expected to hear?

SET-UP: "I sold my house last week. I thought I got a good price for it . . ."
PUNCHLINE: " . . . but it made my landlord mad as hell."

When comedy writers create jokes, they try to be as RIDICULOUS and UNPREDICTABLE as they can be. They deal in a world of the unexpected—things are seldom as they seem. You are expecting a fastball and you are thrown a curve.

BIGGER THAN LIFE

Comedy writers joke about what's real—about the things that happen to people every day. One of our tools is EXAGGERATION. Johnny Carson may have used these simple kinds of exaggeration:

Carson: "I have this friend who is really big."
Ed McMahon: "How big is he?"
Carson: "He is so big his birthday is July 4th, 5th, and 6th."
(OR)
Carson: "My hometown was really conservative."
McMahon: "How conservative was it?"
Carson: "It was so conservative, all the legs of lamb had to be crossed."

Hey, I told you they were simple, so simple, in fact, that I extend my apologies to Johnny and Ed.

Here's a very basic exercise in exaggeration:

"This guy was tough."

"How tough was he?"

"He was so tough, he brushed his teeth with an electric sander." No, he could be tougher (MORE EXAGGERATED):

"He was so tough he brushed his teeth with a street sweeper."

Pretty tough, but could be even tougher (EVEN MORE EXAGGERATED):

"He was so tough he brushed his teeth with dynamite."

Wow, that's TOUGH!

On *Mad About You,* Paul Reiser wouldn't just have a little zit on his face, he'd have "a zit the size of a BUICK."

Now, THAT'S a zit!

SURPRISE, SURPRISE!

When you exaggerate, the result is surprise, and SURPRISE IS THE "KEY" TO HUMOR.

Note how this works in the following:

A man walks into a bar holding a dog he wants to sell. The dog pleads with the bartender—"Please buy me! My owner is mean and nasty, always kicking and hitting me. I'm a great dog. I was in the service—got six medals for bravery. Please buy me!" The bartender is amazed. "How can you sell such a wonderful dog?" he asks the man. And the man says, "Because I am sick and tired of his lies."

Moving right along in the same talking-animal category, I dug up this old chestnut. See if it doesn't sock you with the unexpected:

An Old Man is walking along a country road when he sees a Frog in his path. The Frog tells the Old Man, "If you pick me up and kiss me, I will turn into a beautiful Young Woman and grant your every sexual desire." The Old Man picks up the Frog, puts it in his pocket, and continues walking. "Hey," says the Frog, "you didn't kiss me!"

And the Old Man says, "Well, I thought it over, and at my age I'd rather have a talking frog."

I like this joke. Its logic tickles me. We expect the Old Man to kiss the Frog, and have something silly happen. BUT, a different, ridiculous rug is pulled out from under us, and we reward our surprise with a yuk or two.

FAMILIARITY BREEDS HOO-HA'S

The best jokes are about things we're FAMILIAR with. Universal subjects that people can relate to. Marriage, growing up, relatives, TV, dating, children, work, school, politics, sex, and so on. We identify with these subjects, and then the tables are suddenly turned on us. We are detoured by a surprise. The truth is stretched and exaggerated. What starts out realistically leads us to expect a logical conclusion, but we are tricked! We've been given a mental noogie and we reward that noogie with laughter.

ZINGERS 101

Someone once said that "Dissecting a joke is like cutting open a frog. They both die in the process." That may be true, but at the risk of becoming too clinical, I'd like to explore the various JOKE TECHNIQUES that you have available to you.

Now, don't be overwhelmed by any labels that I may throw at you. Humor is instinctive, off the cuff. When it's funny you know it. I just want you to be aware of how these things work. I want to enhance your position as a comedy "arteest." The more paint colors on your joke brush, the more variety in your humor.

The legendary humorist, Steve Allen, was one of my boyhood comedy heroes. (He still is—but, then again, I refuse to grow up.) Steve Allen and his TV zaniness had a lot to do with my love for comedy. Steve has written many fine books on the subject of humor and its myriad of incarnations. Read him; he will add immeasurably to your comedy education.

Steve would tell you that there are various species of jokes in the world—different schools of comedy—and if you're going to be a successful TV comedy writer, it's a good idea to know how these little chuckle-grabbers work and how they apply to humor on the tube.

The best jokes are those that use a kind of REVERSE thought process. They start out with a logical premise and end with the unexpected. They catch the audience off guard.

Like this one from Jackie Mason:

My grandfather always told me, don't look after your money, look after your health. One day, I was looking after my health, I found out my money was gone. My grandfather took it.

(OR)

Woody Allen reflecting on his boyhood:

My father taught me to swim. He took me out onto the lake in a boat and just threw me overboard. It wasn't half bad once I got out of the sack.

Not what you were expecting, was it? As Gomer Pyle used to say, "Surprise, surprise!"

LITERAL JOKES (taking the literal meaning of one word) always surprise an audience.

QUESTION: "Why was George Washington buried at Mount Vernon?" ANSWER: "Because he was dead." (OR) "Because Mount George was all filled up."

(OR)

"I spilled spot remover on my dog and now I have invisible teeth marks on my leg."

(OR)

"I spilled spot remover on my dog and now something I can't see keeps sticking its tongue up my nose."

(OR)

That eternal question: "If olive oil comes from olives, where does baby oil come from?"

There is a wonderful source of humor in the SIMPLE THINGS we really say:

"Excuse me, are you done eating those fries you threw away?"

(OR)

"Have you finished reading that newspaper you're sitting on?"

A lot of jokes use WORDPLAY, which is exactly what it sounds like (playing with words). Like these Steve Allen favorites:

"See this jacket, it's a seersucker. Sears will sell it to any sucker who comes in."

(OR)

"Here's something that really gets my goat, and you know how painful it is when you're goat's been gotten."

You've heard the term NON-SEQUITOR.—That's when the Punchline has no connection to the Set-Up:

"Anybody who is absent from today's class will be sent home immediately."

(OR)

"A hundred years from now, the works of the Old Masters will be a thing of the past."

Then there's a MALAPROP, an absurd "misuse" of words.

Yankee manager Casey Stengel (to his players): "I want you all to line up in alphabetical order according to size."

(OR)

Movie producer Sam Goldwyn: "A verbal contract isn't worth the paper it's written on."

IMAGERY is an engaging device in comedy. It produces a powerful picture in the audience's mind. It makes them stop for a moment and think. Here's an oldie but goodie to illustrate:

Two men were playing golf. One man was winning, gloating in his victory, and rubbing it in with sarcastic comments. The other man endured it all in silence. In the locker room, the winner collected his money, then noticed that, as the man dressed, he was a priest.

The winner was embarrassed. He said, "Gee, I'm sorry, father. I didn't know you were a priest."

The priest smiled and said, "Yes, I am. Bring your parents to church tomorrow and I'll marry them."

See how imagery works? Saying the punchline without really saying it allows you to fill in a pretty obvious blank, and it's very much in character for the priest.

Another example would be telling someone to stand up when he already IS standing. A pretty great way of telling him he's short.

A DOUBLE ENTENDRE gives a word a double meaning. Like a sign I saw along the Interstate:

"Bernie's Radiator Repair . . . A good place to take a leak."

DEFINITION jokes always make for fun:

Like when Horshack says his name means "The cattle are dying."

(OR)

Bob Hope, aboard ship, entertaining the sailors: "I just got fitted for a navy uniform. You know what a Navy uniform is. It's a girdle with legs."

I've saved PUNS for last because puns have been called the worst form of humor ever created, and that may be true, but they certainly are a great exercise in "wordplay." I don't advocate that you use puns in your writing, unless your character is a compulsive punster who purposely says corny things like:

"Did you hear about the swami who refused novocaine during a root canal? He wanted to transcend dental medication."

The Marx Brothers, along with their writers George S. Kaufman, Morrie Ryskind, Bert Kalmar, and Harry Ruby, developed punstering into an art form. There is nothing I can say about the Marx Brothers that isn't glowing with praise—those zany guys and their writers are American comedy at its highest, punsterish peak.

Kalmar and Ruby, in *Duck Soup,* have Groucho as the leader of a country. When Groucho's minister of war tells him that they should take up the tax, Groucho replies that you can't take up the "tacks" without taking up the carpet. In the same film, Chico turns dollars and taxes into Dallas, Texas, and the word "eliminate" somehow becomes a nice glass of lemonade.

Kaufman and Ryskind, in *Animal Crackers,* have Groucho telling us that the principal animals of the jungle are moose, elk, and the Knights of Pythias. Groucho goes on to inform us that the elks live in the hills and come down every spring for their annual convention, only to be disappointed when they reach the water hole because they were expecting an "elk-a-hole."

My favorite Kaufman/Ryskind line has Groucho saying that he shot an elephant in his pajamas. And how it got in his pajamas he doesn't know.

. . . Oh yeah, Groucho, Chico, Harpo, and sometimes Zeppo demand intense comedy study which is well worth the resulting joy. Surprise! Exaggeration! Silliness! They had it all!

So there you are jokesters, just a few of the wonderful ancient species called "Jokeoramus Yukaluk." There are others, but these should give you a pretty good idea of what's out there for you.

Take a shot at some. It's great fun. And as a learning experience, it sure beats belching up stuffed peppers at three in the morning.

One last thing: If I said, "Is it okay if I join you in a cup of coffee?" what would you say?

THREE JOKES A PAGE

James Komack, the executive producer of *Welcome Back, Kotter,* had a cardinal rule for his writers. You had to have three jokes on every page of your script. Three laughs. As soon as the audience began to stop laughing, they laughed again. Good rule, good producing. Made for a funny, memorable show.

Here's a three-joke page from one of my *Kotter* scripts to illustrate. It's an episode that I wrote with Jewel Jaffe Rannow called "A Love Story." Barbarino is making moves on Epstein's sister, Carmen, and Epstein wants to kill anyone who even looks at his sister. The knowing Gabe Kotter is well aware of what is going on.

INT. CLASSROOM — THE NEXT DAY

CLASS IS IN SESSION. EPSTEIN GLARES AT BARBARINO WHO IS FLIRTING WITH CARMEN.

                    GABE

Vinnie, do you know what love is?

                    BARBARINO

Sure. Love . . . is never havin' to
hear "I'm pregnant."

EPSTEIN

(PLEADS) Please let me kill him,
Mr. Kotter. I'll be gentle, I
promise.

BARBARINO

Juan, you been actin' like a
real nut lately. Is somethin'
the matter?

EPSTEIN

Vinnie, if you believe in the fist
fairy . . . (WAVES FIST) . . . You'll stop
hittin' on my sister.

BARBARINO

I can't do that, Juan. It's not
that I don't wanna, but I can't.
I got this disease . . . "girlitis."
It's like I see a girl and my teeth
automatically flash . . . (THEY DO)
. . . My nostrils automatically flare . . .
(THEY DO) . . . My eyes automatically
twinkle . . .

EPSTEIN

How'd ya like your eyes automatically
black?

See what I mean? Count the jokes. First, Vinnie's definition of love. Then Epstein promises he'll be gentle when he kills Vinnie. "Fist fairy" is not a big joke but it certainly adds color. Vinnie's explanation of girlitis is a good joke "run" for Vinnie. Epstein's retort about a black eye was in rhythm with Vinnie's speech and the audience loved it. This was all on one page, and was successful in meeting the three-joke challenge.

In the same episode, there are more than three jokes in one speech, as Gabe Kotter reflects on the subject of love to his students:

```
                              GABE

                 I remember the first time I ever
                 fell in love. I was five. Babsie
                 was six. I had a thing then for
                 older women. We used to go
                 under the porch and play "doctor."
                 She'd present me with her bill,
                 I'd present her with my bill, we'd
                 sue each other for malpractice . . .
                 for years I thought that was sex.
                 My point is, once I loved Babsie . . .
                 now I love Julie. We're all capable of
                 loving more than once in our lives.
```

I used the three-jokes-a-page concept all the time on *Head of the Class.* Here, in my episode titled "Past Imperfect," the teacher of smart kids, Charlie Moore, learns that he's a few credits short of actual college graduation, so in order to keep his teaching license, he has to take a night course. The only available class is in macroeconomics. It's exam time and Charlie's brain is mush, so his students offer him some tutoring:

```
                              ALAN

                 (TO MR. MOORE) Okay, here's
                 an easy one. What is the
                 equilibrium level of the G.N.P.
                 in an economy in which investment
                 is constant at, say, three hundred
                 dollars and the consumption function
                 is described by 'C' equals one
                 hundred plus zero-point-eight-Y?
```

ALAN HAS WRITTEN (C=100+0.8Y) ON THE BLACKBOARD. HE HANDS THE CHALK TO CHARLIE. CHARLIE STUDIES THE FORMULA FOR A BEAT, THEN:

```
                             CHARLIE

                 (SHRUGS) Could I keep the toaster
                 and come back next week?
```

CHARLIE CHUCKLES. NO ONE SEEMS TO THINK IT'S FUNNY.

                    JAWAHARLAL

     Mister Moore, tell me please, what
     is the Phillips Curve?

                    CHARLIE

     (CAUGHT, THEN QUIPS) It follows
     the Phillips fastball.

                    ERIC

     Does the management of aggregate
     demand through fiscal policy sound
     familiar?

                    CHARLIE

     No.

                    ERIC

     How about the words dead meat?

Review the jokes in this scene. Notice that they're all jokes spun off the subject of economics. Charlie gets a laugh just reacting to Alan's formula. The toaster line scores. So does the baseball retort. And, finally, "dead meat" pretty well sums up a serious situation in a highly descriptive way.

SING ALONG WITH HENNY

A good joke is MUSIC. It flows; it has a certain RHYTHM to it. Too many words—even one too many—can spoil a joke. Here is a textbook example from the crown prince of jokesters, Henny Youngman: "My wife had a facial and she looked gorgeous . . . Three days later, all the mud fell off."

For those of you politically-correct people who don't think jokes about women are funny, consider that, without jokes about women, we wouldn't have jokes about men, and the humor mill would cease to grind out equal opportunity corn.

BUT there is something wrong with Henny's joke. The rhythm is off. There's one word that gets in the way. Take out the word "all" and see how it reads: "My wife had a facial and she looked gorgeous . . . Three days later, the mud fell off."

Well, I don't know about you, but THAT'S music. I can even hear those politically-correctniks emitting a few snorts as they continue to plot against humor.

RAP ALONG WITH RODNEY

In our sport of playing with the language, we must never lose sight of "word placement." Where your KEY word(s) happen to be means everything to the effectiveness of your joke—to whether or not you will get a laugh—or how big that laugh will be.

Picture Rodney Dangerfield saying the following:

I don't know about you, but I've had a pretty rough day. This morning the button on my shirt fell off. Then the heel on my shoe fell off. Then the cap on my tooth fell off . . . Now I'm afraid to go to the bathroom.

Now, if Rodney had said:

I don't know about you, but I've had a pretty rough day. This morning the button FELL OFF my shirt. Then the heel FELL OFF my shoe. Then the cap FELL OFF my tooth . . .

Well, Rodney's whole idea gets muddled. Each sentence, each thought, MUST end with the words FELL OFF so everyone receives the "word picture" you are transmitting. (I apologize for the wee-wee joke, and I assure you it's the only one I know.)

WITH THREE YOU GET HEE-HEE'S

There is an ancient Chinese rumor going around comedy circles that the best sitcom joke has three parts. Very wise. The RULE OF THREE does apply (eggroll extra). It gets us back to words, and how we play with them. The rule of three is a structure for a joke. It's called a TRIPLE. It builds tension, there's a rhythm to it, and it's as easy as this:

I'd like to introduce a man with charm, talent, and wit. Unfortunately, that man can't be here tonight, so we're stuck with Charlie . . .

(OR)

How many Chicagoans does it take to screw in a lightbulb? . . . Three. . . . One to hold the ladder, one to turn the bulb, and one to pay the bribe for the permit.

Okay! So, let's review. A joke is a spontaneous, offbeat way of viewing reality. It's also a very logical way of pointing out the quirky absurdities in life. It presents thoughts in highly unusual ways. Perceives ideas in a manner that no one else has considered before. Absorb this message and you can't lose.

JOKE MAGIC IN HOLLYWOOD

I'll always cherish an incident during my days as a struggling Hollywood actor. An actor friend, Percy Helton, invited me to have lunch with him at the Paramount commissary. We were just about to order when the commissary doors swung open to reveal the unmistakable presence of John Wayne! I swear the man was a thousand feet tall. Wayne made a direct beeline to our table as only John Wayne could beeline. He greeted Percy warmly—they'd worked in umpteen movies together—then Wayne introduced himself to me and asked if he could join us for lunch. I was quick to reply with something that sounded like "Duh . . ."

I had never been a big John Wayne fan, but after having lunch with the man that all changed. Wanna know why? John Wayne was FUNNY. He had a great sense of humor. All through lunch he put things in a funny way and kept us laughing. And I, of course, kept saying, "Duh . . ."

I had never seen this kind of humor in the man on the screen, and he impressed me so much that I went from nonfan to big fan. John Wayne should have done more comedy movies, but then neither Hollywood or his fans would have ever let him do that. At the end of his career, in *True Grit,* he finally got to be funny, and it won him an Oscar.

LAUGHS FROM THE SOUL

People are always telling me jokes. They figure I'm a comedy writer, so they're going to show me that they can be funny too. I'll bet people all around you tell jokes too, but they're usually jokes that have already been created.

A TV comedy writer is not in the business of re-creating other people's humor. A comedy pro is required to CREATE and INI-TIATE humor where it never existed before. To spin out the kind of humor, the kind of jokes, that come OUT OF THE CHARACTERS in the show. When characters say something funny, it should be an off-beat expression of their own point of view. It shows how they see the world, it reveals their attitude. What the characters say gives us clues about who they are.

Study an episode of *Cheers* and notice how the comedy emerges from the characters in the bar. Watch how Frasier Crane will try to intellectualize his way out of a jam—it's a reflection of his char-acter. *Seinfeld*'s George Costanza, on the other hand, is more likely to complain about a problem, then cave in. It's part of his behavior pattern. Kramer will find a way to turn that jam to his advantage. He may be viewed as a screwup, but his supreme confidence (a major Krameresque attitude) makes him a winner, even though he spends most of his time getting other people into trouble.

In *Welcome Back, Kotter*'s "Whodunit?" script, Juan Epstein—who creatively tries to avoid schoolwork of any kind—shows up with a book report that is a month overdue:

> EPSTEIN
>
> (READS) Book report—'The
> Arabian Nights.' Adventure.
> 1942. Black and white. Two
> brothers, Jon Hall, Leif
> Erickson, fight over a throne.
> Maria Montez, Sabu, Turhan
> Bey. Ninety minutes. Repeat.

(EPSTEIN GRINS AT GABE)

Epstein is being very true to his conniving character with a book report that sounds suspiciously like a blurb from *TV Guide*. It got a huge laugh, followed by an even huger second laugh. Why the second laugh? No words—just a grin on Epstein's face that said, "You're buying this, right, Mr. Kotter?"

In "The Puffy Shirt," a terrifically funny *Seinfeld* episode written by Larry David, George Costanza is suddenly offered a job as a hand model. Now, since we are familiar with George's neurotic character, we can assume that he will go overboard, and we are definitely not disappointed. He starts wearing oven mitts to protect his hands. This is the greatest kind of joke because no words are needed. We also see George at his parents' house pampering his newly anointed million-dollar paws. From George's point of view, he is about to rocket to fame as the Fabio of hand models, and, after spending a few maddening moments with George's folks, Frank and Estelle, we can clearly see where George's neuroses took root.

The character of Vice Principal Woodman in *Welcome Back, Kotter* was the perfect foil for Gabe Kotter. Where Gabe was an eternal optimist, Woodman was the supreme pessimist. Where Gabe was a trusting soul, Woodman was a total paranoid. The following excerpt from a two-part episode I wrote with Jewel Jaffe Rannow entitled "Follow The Leader" will clearly illustrate these aspects of Woodman's character:

                         WOODMAN

              What have you been teaching
              your people, Kotter?

                         GABE

              Leadership, Mr. Woodman.

                         WOODMAN

              I used to teach leadership,
              Kotter, and leadership is
              knowing that behind every
              door someone is waiting to
              get you. It's never turning your
              back on a smiling face. They're
              all suckers out there, Kotter.
              Never give them an even break.

Michael Woodman could always be relied on to be a constant kick in the butt for Gabe Kotter.

In my *Head of the Class* script titled "We Love You, Mrs. Russell," the character of "Maria" (a straight-A student) reacts to receiving a failing grade in English.

                         CHARLIE

              Maria, I'm glad I ran into you.
              I have those college catalogs
              you ordered.

                         MARIA

              Keep them! Forget them! Who
              needs them?!

                         CHARLIE

              You do.

```
                    MARIA

         No, I don't. I'm becoming a
         nun and I'll work with homeless
         people in the slums in a land
         ravaged by bandits, pollution,
         corruption, and violence, where
         I'll die much too young and be
         dumped in an unmarked grave
         because no one knew my name!


                   CHARLIE

         Well, at least you're not leaving
         New York.
```

It's no secret that Maria is completely devastated about something and, being a compulsively creative person, she conjures up a worst-case scenario for herself. Charlie Moore, on the other hand, is an excellent teacher, so rather than play into her grief, he uses a joke to loosen her up, so he can get to the root of her problem.

Here's a scene from another *Kotter* script I wrote with Jewel called "Arrividerci, Arnold." Horshack has shown signs of being smart and Woodman has promoted him to a "real" class. Horshack misses his friends and wants to return to the Sweathogs. But how? The following sheds a lot of light on the character of Vinnie Barbarino:

```
                  BARBARINO

         I got it! All you gotta do to
         get sent back is to act dumb.


                  HORSHACK

         Quick thinking, Vinnie! But
         I'd rather not 'act' dumb—
         Something like that has to
         come natural.


                  BARBARINO

         Horshack, I have faith in you.
         It's easy actin' dumb. I do it
         all the time.
```

HORSHACK

I know, Vinnie. You're very good
at it.

BARBARINO

(BLANKLY) What . . . ?

Vinnie's "What . . . ?" speaks volumes about his ability to act dumb. In fact "What?" and "Where?" became national catchwords during Kotter's initial run.

A quick story about Vinnie Barbarino (played by John Travolta). When the first episode of *Kotter* was taped, Vinnie was not only the leader of the Sweathogs, he was smart, he was shrewd, but something wasn't right. The writers made a decision to change Vinnie. Instead of smart, he became vague. Instead of being in control, he started displaying giant flashes of sweetness and vulnerability. The girls screamed. A star was born.

Moving on in our analysis of character, let's rejoin Selma and Guy at *Paradise Shores*. It's nearing the end of the week and their vacations are coming to an end.

SELMA

I had a really great time this
week.

GUY

Yeah, it was fun.

SELMA

So . . . I guess this is it, huh?

GUY

Guess so.

SELMA

Will you write to me?

GUY

I'm a phone person.

SELMA

You'll never call.

GUY

I'll call.

SELMA

No, you won't. You never
asked for my number.

GUY

Okay, what's your number?

SELMA

Apparently, it's zero . . . Look,
all I want to do is get to
know you better.

GUY

Oh, no, you don't—I'm still
in divorce withdrawal—Or as
my lawyer likes to call it,
"whiplash of the mind."

SELMA

I don't have a chance with you,
do I?

GUY

A chance for what?

SELMA

I know I'm not the girl for you—
                    (MORE)

                              SELMA (CONT'D)

          I'm not Ms. Right—big tickets—
          teensy weeny head . . .

                              GUY

          I'm simply not ready to get
          involved, okay? For sixteen
          years, I was half of the team
          of Guy & Pixie.

                              SELMA

          Your ex-wife's name is Pixie? Who
          would name a child Pixie?

                              GUY

          Her mother, Pixie Senior . . . Anyway,
          it's not that I don't like you, I
          DO like you . . .

                              SELMA

          Why?

                              GUY

          . . . Well, you're a very . . . unusual
          person, and I feel . . . Aw, I'm not
          sure what I'm feeling . . . It's
          probably acid reflux.

                              SELMA

          I'll take that as a compliment . . .
          How about if I audition new
          personalities? I'll roll them out—
          you pick the one you like.

SELMA'S HAND SHOOTS UP, STARTS FLAPPING.

                         HAROLD HAND

          (PUPPET VOICE) Good evening, ladies
          and germs—And now, for my first
          impression—Tipper Gore!

                              GUY

          Stop doing that silly stuff . . .

                        HAROLD HAND

          (SAME PUPPET VOICE) Hi, I'm
          Tipper Gore!

                              GUY

          Stop it!

GUY GRABS HER HAND, THEY ARM WRESTLE, HE PINS HER HAND.
A PAUSE AS SHE STARES AT HER LIMP HAND.

                            SELMA

          You killed Tipper.

                              GUY

          (LAUGHS) You're a registered
          foo-foo, y'know that, Selma?
          But, at this moment, I do not
          need you, or any other woman
          in my life!

                            SELMA

          Okay, try THIS on for size!

SELMA LUNGES AND PLANTS A KISS ON GUY'S LIPS.

                              GUY

          What'd you do that for?

                            SELMA

          Couldn't help it. My lips
          are magnetized.

                              GUY

          Geez, you're acting like some
          desperate old maid . . .

GUY STOPS, REALIZING HIS GAFFE. SELMA IS HURT.

                         GUY (CONT'D)

          Look, Selma, I'm sorry for
          flying off like that . . . But
          don't be so anxious . . . I mean,
          I'm sure that someday, some
          fella's gonna give you a
          tumble to the altar.

                            SELMA

          (COOLY) I had hoped to walk there.

SELMA SNATCHES UP HER PURSE.

                         SELMA (CONT'D)

          It is obvious I am not desired in
          this domicile, so I'll just say
          "Aloha" . . . which not only stands for
          "Goodbye," it means "love" . . . I aloha
          you, Guy.

SHE LOOKS PLEADINGLY AT GUY. WHEN HE TURNS AWAY FROM HER,
SHE MARCHES TO THE DOOR, OPENS IT, SLAMS IT SHUT, AND DUCKS
DOWN BEHIND THE SOFA. GUY TURNS TO THE DOOR.

                             GUY

          (BLURTS) Selma, don't go!
          (THEN, SOFTLY TO HIMSELF)
          I'm so alone . . .

Guy and Selma—two lonely "CHARACTERS" looking for love, and finding it.

Hey, it all boils down to one thing: CHARACTER IS TV COMEDY and vice versa. Jokes, emanating from character, tell us a lot about the people we are seeing in our living rooms every week. We laugh at UNIVERSAL character traits like greed, stupidity, selfishness, ego, ad infinitum. (Although a good ad infinitum joke is hard to come up with.) What a sitcom character says usually reflects something that's lurking within every one of us.

JOKES WITHOUT WORDS

Comedy greats like Buster Keaton, Charlie Chaplin, and Harold Lloyd showed very clearly that good comedy doesn't always have to rely on words. The ancient art of mime can often be funnier than words could ever be. But since mime never made it on radio, it's sorely lacking in today's TV comedy shows, which are generally radio with pictures. Today's sitcoms depend entirely too much on words, words, words, ignoring this major form of ACTION humor called PHYSICAL COMEDY.

Most of today's comedy writers are "word dependent." Of course, these writers are often handicapped by the fact that the majority of today's TV comedy performers are "sticks" who can't come close to the physical artistry of Lucille Ball, Jackie Gleason, or Dick Van Dyke. Can you imagine Roseanne doing a physical joke? Hold that thought.

Ellen DeGeneres was an exception—she DID do physical things. The only problem was it was all directly copied from old Lucy bits by a group of verbally addicted writers who were unable to be original in physical terms. An obvious example in one episode had Ellen doing ballet bits just like the ones Lucy did years before.

Martin Lawrence, the star of *Martin,* did an episode where he threw out his back. He didn't need words, his physical moves were wonderful to watch.

Here's an example of physical comedy from a script I penned for a Barbara Eden series called *Harper Valley PTA.* The episode, titled "The Show Must Go On," will not be hard to understand, since it depicts an amateur play being acted out by the Harper Valley Players.

Barbara Eden is "Stella." My ol' buddy George Gobel is "Otis," who is being pursued by a process server. "Wanda" is Stella's rival, who (with her daughter "Scarlett") is trying to sabotage the play. "Bobby" is Wanda's husband who has the hots for Stella. "Dee" is Stella's loyal daughter, and "Buster" is Stella's bumbling, but well-meaning, relative.

The play *(The Curse of the Widow's Heart)* has been written by Stella's rich nemesis, "Flora." And, what was intended as a drama, quickly turns into a farce.

INT. AUDITORIUM STAGE—DAY

OTIS (THE VIKING FATHER) IS WITH STELLA (THE VIKING PRINCESS) IN THE VIKING PALACE.

                    OTIS

          (TO STELLA) Yumpin' Yimminy!
          Your soldier is a faithless man.
          I am about to receive information
          that he is already married to another
          . . . I sure hope the messenger arrives
          soon, the hurricane season is upon
          us.

ANGLE ON WANDA-IN THE WINGS

SHE CHUCKLES TO HERSELF AS SHE CRAWLS ALONG, REMOVING THE SUPPORT BRACES FROM THE PALACE WALL FLAT . . . A BEAT, DEE CRAWLS INTO VIEW, REPLACING THE BRACES . . . A BEAT, SCARLETT, CHUCKLING TO HERSELF, CRAWLS INTO VIEW, TAKING THE BRACES OUT AGAIN. BEHIND SCARLETT, BUSTER RATTLES A LARGE PIECE OF SHEET METAL TO SIMULATE THUNDER.

ANGLE - ONSTAGE

                    STELLA

          (TO OTIS) I fear not the hurricane—
          strong winds will carry me to my
          true love's arms.

ANGLE ON BUSTER-IN THE WINGS

HE HITS A MASTER SWITCH, AND THE ROOM FANS HE HAS NAILED TO A PIECE OF PLYWOOD START TO BLOW!

ANGLE—ONSTAGE

THE FANS ARE SO STRONG THAT THEY BLOW OVER THE FLAT, BLOW STELLA INTO OTIS'S ARMS, AND BLOW BOTH OF THEM ONTO THE BED.

ANOTHER ANGLE—ONSTAGE

BUSTER AND A FEW OF THE CREW QUICKLY PUT THE FLAT BACK UP. THE AUDIENCE LAUGHS, APPLAUDS, AND BUSTER CAN'T HELP BUT TAKE A LITTLE BOW.

BACK TO STELLA & OTIS—ONSTAGE

THEY ARE SPRAWLED ACROSS THE BED.

                        OTIS

            It looks like the hurricane
            season is here.

A <u>KNOCK</u> ON THE DOOR. OTIS QUICKLY ANSWERS, THROWS OPEN THE
DOOR, AND IS HIT IN THE FACE WITH A PAIL OF WATER.

                    OTIS (CONT'D)

            Yup, it's hurricane season all
            right.

A <u>HAND</u> APPEARS THROUGH THE DOORWAY, HANDING OTIS A PAPER.
OTIS TAKES THE PAPER, CLOSES THE DOOR, AND CROSSES BACK TO
STELLA IN TRIUMPH.

                    OTIS (CONT'D)

            I now have the incriminating
            evidence against your lover—
            Information that will most
            certainly send him to prison.
            (READS PAPER, REACTS) This is
            a summons for ME . . . !

OTIS REACTS, HIS MUSTACHE FALLS OFF, THE AUDIENCE LOVES IT.

ANGLE ON FLORA—IN THE AUDIENCE

AS SHE SLOWLY SHREDS HER PROGRAM.

INT. AUDITORIUM STAGE—LATER IN THE PLAY

THE SCENE IS THE SOLDIER'S SHABBY ROOM. A KNOCK AT THE DOOR,
WHICH COMPLETELY FALLS OFF ITS HINGES, REVEALING AN
EMBARRASSED STELLA.

ANGLE ON WANDA—IN THE WINGS

LAUGHING HYSTERICALLY AS SHE FLAPS TOGETHER THE DOOR HINGES
IN HER HANDS.

ANGLE—ONSTAGE

BOBBY (THE SOLDIER) GOES TO EMBRACE STELLA:

                    BOBBY

        My love, you have return-ed!

BOBBY TRIES TO KISS HER.

                    STELLA

        No, cad, no!

STELLA PUSHES BOBBY SO HARD, HE IS PROPELLED ACROSS AND
RIGHT OFF THE BED.

                 STELLA (CONT'D)

        You have wrong-ed me and had
        a child by another.

                    BOBBY

        What folly is this?

STELLA MOVES TO A CRIB—POINTS DOWN.

                    STELLA

        THIS baby which lies here!

                    BOBBY

        (JOINS HER) What baby is that?

                    STELLA

        This . . . !

STELLA REALIZES THERE IS NO BABY. SHE BEGINS A FRANTIC
SEARCH THROUGH THE CRIB.

                 STELLA (CONT'D)

        Well, there's gotta be a baby
        here somewhere!

ANGLE ON BUSTER—IN THE WINGS

SEARCHING THE PROP TABLE FOR THE PROP DOLL. HE SEES WANDA
HOLDING THE DOLL, AND A TUG-OF-WAR BEGINS. BUSTER CAPTURES
THE DOLL (EXCEPT FOR ONE LEG WHICH WANDA STILL HOLDS).
BUSTER TOSSES THE DOLL UP OVER THE FLAT.

ANGLE—ONSTAGE

STELLA CATCHES THE DOLL.

                          STELLA

              (TO BOBBY) THIS baby!

THE AUDIENCE LAUGHS.

                      STELLA (CONT'D)

              I have but one thing to say
              to you, and it is this . . .
              (FORGETS HER LINES) . . . it's,
              uh . . . uh . . .

ANGLE ON BUSTER—IN THE WINGS

                          BUSTER

              (LOUD WHISPER ONSTAGE) Your
              lines are on the baby!

ANGLE—ONSTAGE

STELLA TURNS THE DOLL EVERY WHICH WAY, FINALLY READING ITS
REAR.
                          STELLA

              "Made by the Hong Kong Doll
              Company."

THE AUDIENCE LAUGHS, STELLA CONTINUES.

                      STELLA (CONT'D)

              (READING UNDER DOLL'S ARM) "I
              have come to rid my world of
              evil."

STELLA DROPS THE DOLL INTO THE CRIB, PULLS OUT A TOY PISTOL, AIMS IT AT BOBBY, AND PULLS THE TRIGGER.

> STELLA (CONT'D)
>
> Take that!

NO GUNSHOT. STELLA PULLS THE TRIGGER AGAIN.

> STELLA (CONT'D)
>
> And that!

NO GUNSHOT. THINKING QUICKLY, STELLA SEIZES BOBBY'S SWORD.

> STELLA (CONT'D)
>
> Then you shall die by the sword!

STELLA POKES BOBBY, AND THE RUBBER SWORD BENDS. THINKING EVEN MORE QUICKLY, STELLA HOLDS OUT HER FIST.

> STELLA (CONT'D)
>
> All right, I will kill you with
> my poison ring!!

STELLA PLUNGES HER RING FINGER AT BOBBY'S HEART. A "GUNSHOT" IS HEARD. BOBBY FALLS INTO A HEAP. STELLA DOES A TAKE AT THE RING, AND THE AUDIENCE IS HYSTERICAL.

ANGLE ON WANDA—IN THE WINGS

GLEEFULLY BLOWING IMAGINARY SMOKE FROM THE DUPLICATE TOY PISTOL SHE HOLDS.

ANGLE—ONSTAGE

STELLA PUTS HER FOOT ON BOBBY'S DEAD BODY, AND DELIVERS THE MORAL:

> STELLA
>
> Father was right—never trust
> a poor person.

THE LIGHTS DIM. THE AUDIENCE APPLAUDS AND CHEERS.

Wasn't that fun? I love sight gags, and I certainly had great time writing this. I even included the old "poison ring" bit because this was the perfect spot for it. I just chucked it out of that enormous joke file I call my noggin.

By the way, the best part of working with Barbara Eden was Barbara Eden. Beautiful. Gracious. The ultimate pro. The Monday morning script reading was always bright when I got to sit next to and dream of "Jeannie."

Now, you may have noticed that old Jer (who said never use camera angles), used camera angles again in the above scene. Well, my excuse this time is that *Harper Valley PTA* wasn't TAPE, it was shot on FILM. This being the case, the style was more cinematic, and the fast action of the scene certainly demanded it. (This excuse clearly illustrates another reason why you should try to locate a sample script from the show you are writing your spec script for.)

So, summing up, I believe there should be much more physical comedy (or "schtick" as the Greeks called it) in today's sitcoms. The funniest moments in theatre, movies, and TV will always be those that don't rely on words. Sight gags are actually easier than verbal comedy for audiences to comprehend. They need no language, they're universal. Everyone laughs at a person slipping on a banana peel. It looks funny and, since it's not happening to us, it's hysterical! Rent a movie with Peter Sellers as Inspector Jacques Clouseau and have yourself a ball.

LIFE OR DEATH OF A SALESPERSON

As you stand there, warmly embracing your newly improved, completely edited script, you're probably flushed all over with pride as you think to yourself: "At last, my work is done."

Well, that's a pretty nice thought, but not at all true. Now that you have your script—your key to the door of sitcom success—you are well along on your journey. Well, at least halfway along. It's time to SELL what you have written, to throw your "baby" out there and see if it will fly. This is where your script earns its wings.

The process of MARKETING a script is a collaboration between you, a copy machine, the phone company, and the U.S. Postal Service. It can either be a pleasurable experience or one that makes you feel like you're submerged in a tank full of sharks, dressed as a ham hock.

THE SAFE SIDE

This leads us to the first phase in the marketing procedure—PRO-TECTION. By all means, protect your material before you send it out to anyone—and especially before you let your no-good brother-in-law, Louie, read it. Have proof that you (and not Louie) are the creator of the work.

A teleplay cannot be copyrighted. In television, the purchaser, not the creator becomes the owner. I know, it's a lousy deal, but that's the way it is. Maybe someday justice will prevail, but for now this is what we're stuck with.

You can protect your script by REGISTERING it with the Writers' Guild of America west. Nonmembers of the Guild are allowed to register their material, so here's what you have to do:

Send your script (unbound) in a sturdy envelope that won't let it get pulverized by postal employees to: Writers' Guild of America west, 7000 West Third Street, Los Angeles, CA 90048 (Attn: Registration Department). Enclose a check for $20 made out to WGAw. No checkee, no registree. You will receive a dated registration receipt from the Guild that will protect your script for five years. Registrations are renewable. There is a Writers' Guild of America east office in New York, but for TV I recommend the LA office. If you have any questions, call the WGAw Registration Department at (323) 782-4500.

A second way you can protect your script is by mailing it to yourself, and filing it away, unopened, in the dated envelope. This is not an absolutely foolproof method because there have been recent court actions in which some legal cretins have challenged it, but do it anyway. It couldn't hurt.

THE PROOF IS IN THE PACKAGING

Marketing a script is like marketing a product, so make that product as attractive and professional-looking as possible. This means a neatly typewritten copy with NO crossouts. Any changes require new printed pages. The pages of your script should be on three-holed paper, and attached with metal brads. The composition of each page should be in the proper format. A failure to do these things will instantly mark you as a blabbering fool. Covers are optional—nothing fancy with calligraphy or hummingbirds—a heavy, colored paper with no printing on it will suffice.

The first thing a reader should see is your TITLE PAGE, with your name, address, and phone number at the bottom left of the page.

(Add fax and e-mail if applicable.) I have received "spec" scripts without addresses and phone numbers—scripts I liked—but I didn't know where the people were or how to find them. Too bad—this simple omission forced these people to forget about their dreams of creativity and settle for government jobs.

Now, I know I've already mentioned this, but I cannot stress it enough: Please NUMBER your pages! You'd be surprised at how many people forget to do this, and the reason for doing this should be obvious. If the reason for doing this is not obvious, I hear there are careers available for pinsetters at your local bowling chalet.

Make as many copies of your script as you'll want to send out, and keep two or more copies for yourself. If you work at a computer, store your script on a disk. NEVER have just one copy of your script, and NEVER, EVER give your only copy to someone. You worked long and hard to turn out this baby, and you don't want some nerfball boo-boo to negate a future that includes a big house with a parrot and a jacuzzi the size of Cleveland.

SHIP IT

Okay, your script looks great—it's protected—you're ready to send it out. But who do you send it out to? Good question. Glad you asked.

First, a few SUGGESTIONS:

1. DON'T send it out unsolicited. You'll get it back unopened (if you get it back at all).
2. DON'T send it directly to studios, shows, or production companies (unless you have a contact there).
3. DO send it to an AGENT. The TV sitcom business works on an agent system. A writer MUST be represented by an agent.
4. CALL the agent before sending out your material. Find out if the agent will read a script by a new writer. Some will, some won't. Some require a signed release before opening the envelope. A release is a protection device for the agent, in case the agent is dealing with a mentally defective writer with a gun collection.

ABOUT TEN-PERCENTERS

By now you're probably wondering to yourself, "Where do I find these agents?" I knew you were going to ask that, so turn to the back of this book and check out the agent list in APPENDIX A.

If you want even more information, or a more complete agent list, call the Writers' Guild of America west Agency Department at (323) 782-4502. There may be a small fee for the list, and when you receive it you'll see that it's a pretty lengthy piece of work, which will cause you to wonder who the devil all these agents are.

So, here are some AGENT POINTERS:

1. Eliminate any agency that does not work out of the Los Angeles area. An agent in Idaho may be very good for a script about potatoes, but the agents with strong TV comedy connections are in L.A.
2. It's a long list, you may not have any idea of who's who, so go for the biggies first. CAA, ICM, United Talent, William Morris. Who knows? Maybe you'll break through.
3. If you happen to know which agents represent most of the working sitcom writers, these are the agents you should be trying to get through to. These are the people with the real clout in the TV racket. These are the people in appendix A.
4. Never associate with an agent who asks you for a reading fee, or any money at all.
5. Forget about the agent who requests more than a 10 percent commission. Ten percent is standard in the industry. It's why agents are called "ten-percenters."
6. Avoid any agent with the last name of Hitler.

THE WAITING GAME

It's a good idea to send your script out to more than one agent. The process takes time—certain agents will be slow in getting back to you, others may be quick with a rejection, some you'll never hear from at all. But, generally, it's a waiting game. A watching for the mail—waiting by the phone, the fax, the e-mail—sort of ritual.

If certain agents haven't responded after a period of time, give those agents a call to inquire about your script. It's not always necessary to speak directly to the agent. The assistant who answers the phone can probably answer your questions. That person may very likely be the one who actually reads your script, so get friendly. Start a long-distance relationship. That assistant may run a network one day.

It's easier to deal with this waiting period if you're busy working on another script, or some other writing project. Always have another bun in your mental oven—it prevents you from becoming obsessed with the slow pace of the marketing process. You'll get rejections, so bounce back. Keep going!

PAYDIRT!

Wonder of wonders! Can it be? An agency calls—they LOVE your script! Get out that stupid jester hat; it's party time again! You should realize, however, that at this point you haven't actually sold your script. You have an agent—someone who is going to represent you. Someone who is going to send your script to TV comedy producers, story editors, and production companies as a "sample" of your writing talent. These people are always looking for new writers, and the hope is that one of these people will be intrigued enough with the comic genius of your writing, that he will want to meet with you in person!

Let's say your script has caught the interest of the producer of a new, hit comedy show. The producer will probably tell you your script is great. It would get an Oscar if they gave out Oscars for sitcom. The producer will want to get together with you as soon as possible. If you don't live in the Los Angeles area, this will mean a trip to Tinseltown at your own expense, but think of all the gigantic checks that loom in your future. Be positive. Take action. A major door has opened for you. Welcome to Hollywood.

Now, it is highly unlikely that this interested party will buy your "spec" script outright. Your script is a SALES TOOL—a calling card into the industry—a ticket to ride on the Yellow Brick Road. It took me a year and a half and a great deal of tenacity to convince my bosses at *Love, American Style* to actually produce the spec script that got me the job.

The day of your meeting you'll gather with the producer, and probably a few staff writers, and the first question you will hear is: "What else have you got?" They liked your script—it showed you can tell a story and be funny—so what other ideas do you have?

YAKETTY-YAK

Sitcom story ideas have to be marketed VERBALLY to producers and/or staff writers. In show biz, this is known as the PITCH. The pitch was invented because executives in the television business don't read (their lips can't move that fast). Whether this is true or not is up for generous speculation. One thing I DO know—besides the writing itself—pitching is the most grueling experience a writer is expected to undergo.

Anyhow, they want to hear your ideas. This means your meeting is going to be a PITCH session, so be prepared to talk your little heart out. And never appear desperate. You've got them right where they want you.

I've always preferred pitching story ideas to a relatively new show, but writers don't always have that luxury, and it's a major challenge pitching ideas for a show that has been on the air for five or more seasons. The feeling is they've done everything and there's an "Okay, show me" attitude that the producer and staff writers convey when you attempt to present your ideas. Don't let this throw you— these people are desperate for you to succeed. A compelling story idea from you is going to keep them on the air and continue to pay the mortgages on their overpriced beach houses. You are important to the economics of show business.

The following scene will give you some idea of what a pitch meeting is like:

INT. TV PRODUCER'S OFFICE - DAY

(JERRY NERVOUSLY FIDGETS, SEATED OPPOSITE BIG-TIME TV
PRODUCER, MANNY GLASS. THE SITCOM IS ABOUT THOSE MECHANICAL
FUNSTERS—"THE BLEEP FAMILY." IT'S THE HONEYMOONERS, ONLY
THEY'RE ALL ROBOTS. THE SHOW IS GOING INTO ITS SEVENTH
SEASON.)

                              GLASS

          (TO JERRY) So, whaddya got?

                              JERRY

          (CHECKS NOTES) Well, uh, Ralph
          loses his job at the nuclear
          power plant, and . . .

                              GLASS

          (INTERRUPTS) We did that.

                              JERRY

          Uh, okay, Ed and Trixie are
          mistaken for junk on recycling
          day . . .

                              GLASS

          (INTERRUPTS) We did that.

                              JERRY

          Okay . . . how about this? Ralph
          loses his membership in the
          Tincan Lodge when he gets mad
          and calls the head Tincan a
          rust bucket . . .

                              GLASS

          A robot wouldn't say that.

                              JERRY

          (A BIT BEWILDERED) How do you
          know a robot wouldn't say that?

                              GLASS

          'Cause I'm a genius. What else
          ya got?

                    JERRY

        All right, here's my "A" idea.
        Ralph is . . .

(JERRY STOPS, IS SILENT)

                    GLASS

        What didya stop for?

                    JERRY

        I was waiting for you to say,
        'We did that.'

                    GLASS

        Don't be a smartass, I'll say
        we did that when I think we
        did that. What else ya got?

                    JERRY

        Okay, picture this . . . Ralph is
        jealous because Ed is attracted
        to Alice's magnetism.

                    GLASS

        I love it! Unfortunately, it's
        already in development.

(GLASS SPRINGS OUT OF HIS CHAIR, USHERS JERRY TO THE DOOR)

                GLASS (CONT'D)

        Nice try, kid. Get some more
        ideas, we'll talk.

                    JERRY

        But . . .

(GLASS SLAMS THE DOOR IN JERRY'S FACE. THEN GLASS GRINS,
THINKS TO HIMSELF . . .)

GLASS

Hmmm . . . Attracted by her magnetism
. . . I smell Emmy.

The previous scene is a little exaggerated, but not too far from the truth. And the truth is TV comedy writing is basically a sales medium, which allows wide latitude for theft. I mean, try to prove you pitched that idea. Are you about to sue Warners? How about ABC? UPN? Professional suicide. We all know there is no blacklist in show business, but you keep off that imaginary list by never screwing the biggies, even though the biggies are allowed to screw you.

Now, since the verbal pitch is the biggest step in making a sale, it only follows that the best salespeople are the most successful writers. Many talented writers are introverted. They have trouble expressing themselves verbally, so they don't sell and end up teaching Chaucer to drill-press majors at the local technical school.

Luckily, my acting background came in handy, as I always "acted" the role of the writer who was going to sell a story. This gave the impression that I was a crack salesman, which usually led to a sale. Shakespeare was an actor, probably a very good actor. I mean, look at all the stuff he sold.

I feel very strongly that all TV writers should take courses in acting and public speaking. These tools are just as important as writing skills, and you'll find them invaluable when you deliver your EMMY acceptance speech.

PITCH STRATEGY

Go into a pitch meeting as if you know what you're doing. It works for the president, it can work for you. Have at least three story ideas—each idea worked out with a BEGINNING (the problem), MIDDLE (complicating the problem), and END (problem resolved). Be prepared with a quick, one-line, *TV Guide*–type synopsis of each idea in case the producer is hung over and late for his AA meeting.

Smile a lot. It makes you appear confident. Even if you've been in a domestic quarrel and have a bullet lodged in your forehead, SMILE! Funny people are expected to smile, so this is no time for dour. Woody Allen probably turns into Jim Carrey when he pitches.

SPITBALLS are good weapons to bring into a pitch meeting. Spitballs are little "wild card" thoughts that you use if your other stuff is taking a dive. A well-placed spitball has often saved me from a complete nosedive.

ROBOTS 'R ME

Once, in one of my non-network periods, I pitched story ideas to a syndicated show called *Small Wonder,* about a family bringing up a little girl robot. Honest.

Well, my three story pitches went down in flames. Everything I put out there was kicked and beaten senseless. The producer even hated the shoes I was wearing. I had no recourse but to pitch a spitball.

I said, "Okay, what if the family is watching *The Wizard of Oz* on TV and the little robot girl asks her family for a heart?" SALE!! The only drawback was I had to go home and figure out how the hell I was going to support this spitball brilliance with a decent story. But, somehow, I managed and I'm still getting residuals today!

Remember that word—RESIDUALS. We'll discuss it later. A very inspirational topic.

HAPPY DAYS

One of my more curious pitching experiences occurred when I presented story ideas to the classic sitcom, *Happy Days*. It was while I was story editor on *Love, American Style. Happy Days* was also on the Paramount lot, and in-studio incest was encouraged.

Happy Days was going into its first season, so the show was in the initial development stage. When I walked into the story editor's office, I was met by a gruff, humorless man who very likely tortured squirrels as a hobby. I could tell this by the buck-toothed little heads mounted on his wall.

STORY EDITOR

```
Look, this is a show about this
white bread kid named Richie
Cunningham who goes to high
school in Wisconsin, where
he hangs out with his funny
family and nutty friends.
Think you can handle
that . . . ?
```

SCORE! Game over! Victory was mine! Sometimes you're in the right place at the right time, and this was definitely my right time and right place. I was a white-bread kid who went to high school in Wisconsin. I had a funny family and nutty friends. I WAS Richie Cunningham!

The story editor seemed pleased to hear this. It was hard to tell because he never smiled. He looked like Ebenezer Scrooge on a bad hemorrhoid day. I imagined that, since this guy was from New York City, he only recently learned that there actually was a Wisconsin. (To people in show business, the United States consists of New York City, Los Angeles, and the stuff in the middle that you fly over.)

Anyhow, I think I caught Mr. Scrooge off-guard because he caved in and said he was interested in one of my story ideas. Then, he told me a bit more about the show.

STORY EDITOR

```
We've got this character named
"Fonzie" . . . You don't have
to put him in your story if you
don't want to. We're not sure
he's gonna work out.
```

Today, that story editor has a rosary business in Tel Aviv.

BOO-HOO

Whenever you pitch story ideas to a comedy show, you face rejection. You have opened yourself up to being kicked in the head on a regular basis. The companies which turn out these half-hour sausages are rife with insecurity. Cancellation is always looming and they are very reluctant to put their fortunes in the hands of a newcomer unless, of course, it's a relative.

As practical career choices go, TV comedy writer ranks right up there with wrangler on an ant farm. If you're looking for security, get a job at the local prison. Not to mention the competition factor. My God, the membership of the Writers' Guild numbers over eight thousand. Luck is with you, however, since only a handful of these writers have any real talent.

RESILIENCE AND TENACITY

In the entertainment game, the rejection quotient for actors is higher than for writers. And when an actor is rejected, it's physical, which is why so many actors have new noses. A writer, on the other nose, can just think up another story. It's not easy (especially after that nose line), but you do it because you're RESILIENT—you refuse to quit! You've learned how to bounce back from disappointment, and you put your nose back on the line. (I did it again. Sorry.)

Along with resilience goes TENACITY—the ability to keep going, to forge ahead. TENACITY AND RESILIENCE ARE THE TWO MOST IMPORTANT EMOTIONAL KEYS IN ESTABLISHING A SUCCESSFUL WRITING CAREER.

As a struggling writer, you have only one ally—yourself—but you can be your own worst enemy as well. If you're going to take rejection personally—if you're going to let it stop your creative flow—put this book down. You don't have the guts for this business.

If you DO have the guts for this business, and you possess the will to persevere, there are financial rewards that can make the whole trip worthwhile. They pay TV writers a lot of money. They have to. The Betty Ford Center is very expensive.

If it makes the journey any easier, always keep in mind that TV comedy writing is an occupation in which you often have to prove your talent to people who have none, so since you hold the upper hand, it's up to you to lead the way.

YAHOO

If, in the middle of your pitch, the producer jumps up and says, "Wow!" it could mean one of two things:

1. He's about to buy the most brilliant story he's ever heard, or . . .
2. His Ex-Lax finally kicked in.

If it's (hopefully) number one, congratulations! You just opened another major door. You are about to be asked to join a very exclusive club of writers who actually get paid for writing. This means the scriptwriting process will start all over again, and you are on your way to winning $18,000, plus residuals if the show produces enough episodes to make reruns financially viable.

We'll discuss residuals later—a riveting subject.

ALL TALK, NO WRITE

There is one particular downside to this whole practice of the verbal pitch, one that I have often encountered when writers pitched to me. It seems that a lot of individuals are wonderfully amusing talkers, but they can't write worth sewer slush. Unfortunately, this is not evident as they pitch. Many of these writers have talked their ways to great success in show business. The higher up they move, the less they have to write, so they become producers and soon find themselves relying solely on writers with talent to make them into rich geniuses . . . Just one of the many survival tactics employed in the mysterious world of yuks for money.

It's Perfect! I Love It! Do It Over!

Well, you've done it. They bought that crazy idea of yours. I am so proud of you. You've rocketed head-first through another major door. This means, of course, that the scriptwriting steps you used to guide you through your "spec" script will now begin anew as you, once again, frolic through the stages of:

1. Story Synopsis
2. Story Outline
3. First Draft
4. Second Draft
5. Fame, Fortune, and Tax Breaks

Now, during numbers 1 through 4, and before achieving number 5, you will be asked to do "Oh, just some minor REWRITES."

You'll have script meetings between the above-mentioned stages where you will undergo various critiques of your work. These meetings usually begin with:

"We love what you did, we only have a few NOTES . . ."
So, be aware of the following:

1. You are about to receive some "constructive" criticism—
   changes that those with seniority over you believe will
   improve your work. Take careful, detailed notes on their
   notes. I know it's not always easy to bend, nor should you
   always be willing to be bent. By all means, defend your
   material, your point of view. Be ready to explain why your
   way is the best way. You'll be surprised at how reasonable
   people can be when they're not insane.
2. The notes you receive from those in charge may be logical
   and intelligent but, as valid as their criticisms are, watch
   out for their "solutions"; they may border on lunacy. Tell
   them you'd like to take your own shot at figuring out how
   to incorporate any changes.
3. It's possible that you will go through a writer's version of
   "Hell Week," where one small suggestion will change the
   entire direction and complexion of your story. Suddenly,
   Vincent Price has gone mad and is lowering you into a vat
   of piping hot wax as you're asked to change the dog to a
   moose, the wedding to a funeral, the priest to an exotic
   dancer. Certain "small" suggestions like these may quite
   possibly destroy the entire structure of your script, so be
   cautious.

Here's where you have to stand your ground. Here's where you'll start
to wonder two OTHER things:

1. If they're having so many problems with my story, why
   did they buy the stupid thing in the first place? and
2. Where are these cockamamie NOTES coming from?

I once received a script note from a producer that began, "My maid
had trouble with the first act . . ." My career flashed before me as I felt
Vincent sliding me into that piping hot wax.

THE FLEXIBILITY ABILITY

Warning: It's counterproductive to get all jerked out of shape over the notes you receive on your writing efforts. Sure, you've committed to what you've written. You should be committed. But beware of forming unreasonably rigid and unhealthy attachments to your golden words and ideas. Fight to remain OBJECTIVE. Be willing to explore new avenues, streets, boulevards, pathways, trails, highways, byways, and this sentence is getting much too long . . .

Anyhow, take a good, long look at your own suspicions before you go public. If certain things in your story or script are bothering you, acknowledge what you're feeling. If you don't address these things, somebody else will definitely be there to do it for you.

Keep in mind that each day you awake as a better, more experienced writer, so you have every right to take it upon yourself to question the judgment of your past.

Rewrites are a traditional part of the sitcom writing process, so never be afraid or reluctant to change things—welcome the opportunity. Don't be defensive and act as if they're sticking pins in your baby. Be aware that this is all geared to go in your favor and, after all, the only goal of all parties should be to turn out the best script possible. What's on the screen is all that counts.

Let's say you're writing a script for a new, hot show called *Crazy in Love* about a twentysomething couple (Brad and Janet) who are crazy in love, hence the title.

Here's a sample of the scene you might have written:

```
               BRAD

     I love you, Janet, I really do.
     With all my heart. I think about
     you all the time. Wherever I go,
     I see your face. At night, I toss
     and turn thinking of you. I can't
     get you out of my mind . . . So,
     will you mmmm . . . (CAN'T GET IT
     OUT) . . . Will you mmmm . . .
     mmmmm . . .
```

```
(JANET WHACKS HIM ON THE BACK)

                    BRAD (CONT'D)

(BLURTS OUT)—MARRY ME!!

                    JANET

(COOS COYLY) Why, Brad, what a surprise.
```

Okay, pretend I'm your producer, and I'm giving you notes on this little scene. I think it's a nice little scene—says what you want to say. I like the coy cooing thing with Janet at the end. BUT. "But what?" you ask with trepidation. "But it needs to be a lot funnier," I continue. "Make it cuter. Tell me more about these characters."

So, you take another look at it, swish it around in your brain. Maybe you decide to play more with the emotions—explore Brad's nervousness and Janet's anticipation—which will allow for more byplay between these two lovestruck young people. Your rewrite may look something like this:

```
                    BRAD

(NERVOUSLY TO JANET) Janet, I . . .
I . . . I . . . I . . .

                    JANET

(INTERRUPTS) Enough with the I,
I, I's, Brad. You sound like Desi
Arnaz.

                    BRAD

Look, Janet, what I'm trying to
say is that I love you . . . Really I
do . . . Honest . . . I'm sure I do . ..
I mean, I'm pretty sure I do . . .

                    JANET

(INTERRUPTS AGAIN) You can stop
while you're ahead, Brad.
```

                         BRAD

          All night I toss and turn, and
          it's more than that hamstring
          I pulled playing squash . . . What
          I'm trying to say is I can't get
          you out of my mind. Wherever I go,
          I see your face. This morning, I
          told my boss I loved him.

                         JANET

          So, are you guys, like, having a thing?

                         BRAD

          Janet, I'm serious . . . Will you
          mmmm . . .(CAN'T GET IT OUT) . . .
          Will you mmmm . . .mmmmm . . .

(JANET WHACKS HIM ON THE BACK)

                    BRAD (CONT'D)

          (BLURTS OUT)—MARRY ME!!

                         JANET

          (COOS COYLY) Why, Brad, what a surprise.

Speaking as your pretend producer, I am very pleased. I love what
you've done. You fleshed out the scene—put a funnier spin on it. It
tells us more about the characters. Excellent work. Just one little note:
It's much too long. CUT it.

        Well, thanks to that charming, insightful producer of yours,
you are almost there. And with some judicious EDITING, this could
likely be the result:

                         BRAD

          (NERVOUSLY) Janet, I love you.
          Really I do . . . I'm sure I do . . .
          I mean, I'm pretty sure I do . . .

                    JANET

        (INTERRUPTS) You can stop while
        you're ahead, Brad.

                    BRAD

        Look, what I'm trying to say is
        I can't get you out of my mind.
        Wherever I go, I see your face.
        This morning, I told the clerk
        at the doughnut shop I loved him.

                    JANET

        It'll never work out—he's a
        Methodist.

                    BRAD

        Janet, I'm serious . . . Will you mmmm . . .
        (CAN'T GET IT OUT) . . . Will you mmmm . . .
        mmmmm . . .

(JANET WHACKS HIM ON THE BACK)

                    BRAD

        (BLURTS OUT)—MARRY ME!!

                    JANET

        (COOS COYLY) Why, Brad, what a surprise.

Hey, it works for me. Some nifty editing you did there, and notice
how you continued to rewrite in the process . . .

        Now, put your script down for a day and look at it with fresh
eyes tomorrow, when you'll likely find yourself rewriting once again.
Personally, I always look forward to rewriting my writing. It gives me
a shot at polishing that rock into a diamond.

REWRITES IN THE NIGHT

One day soon, when your superb writing has landed you on the writing staff of a sitcom, you will find yourself dealing with rewrites all the time. You'll be required to do quick fixes on a daily basis.

Now, the writing staff of your average sitcom consists of anywhere from four to, maybe, eight scribes, sometimes more. A team counts as ONE, and is paid that way, challenging the belief that two heads are better.

The producer(s) are usually writers too, so they add to this number. This way the show has more coverage in its most important area which is, in case you haven't caught on by now, the WRITING.

Some staff writers work short days; for others it's a seven-day-a-week grind. It depends on how organized the boss is, and how efficiently things get done.

A question I'm frequently asked is: "Do all the writers sit around a table and write the scripts?" And my answer is:

NO! Please! Never! Allowing an assorted bunch of comedy zanies to construct a single script with a unifying idea would be like hiring The Three Stooges to build the Hoover Dam. It's not easy getting a group of writers to speak as one.

This being the case, each writer on the staff writes his own scripts, gets rewrite notes from the others, and this seems to work out just fine. Staff writers also work with freelancers, giving them rewrite notes and helping them to develop their ideas into stories and scripts.

Where the "writers' roundtable" comes into play is when a show is in production. The script that is being produced that week is suddenly the property of every writer on the staff. Not everything is going to work, which means it's time for . . . REWRITES.

The three-to-five-day production week begins with the show's entire staff gathering around a table where the actors read through the script for the first time. Those weeks when it was my script on the block, I was generally sedated with a tire iron. Every precious joke had to score, and when they preciously bombed, it was time for . . . REWRITES.

After the reading, the writing staff assembles around that roundtable and starts throwing out lines, frantically attempting to create boffo jokes to replace the ones relegated to laugh limbo. It's very competitive in that room with every jokester trying to out-joke every other jokester. There is no democracy. The head guy (executive producer) generally decides what goes in and what doesn't, but the result is usually a much funnier script.

That is . . . until late afternoon the next day, when the writers assemble on the soundstage to watch the actors run through yesterday's rewritten teleplay. This visual aid may likely reveal more "holes" to be filled—not only jokes, but possibly entire scenes that are not working. This means it's time for . . . REWRITES. Sometimes late into the night. The actors have to have a freshly revised script in the morning.

The rewriting process continues throughout the entire rehearsal period. By the on-camera dress rehearsal, hopefully everyone is satisfied. If not, it's time for . . . REWRITES.

Once, during the taping of a *Welcome Back, Kotter* episode, the first of two live audience shows did not score as well as we thought it would. This meant it was time for . . . REWRITES. The crack *Kotter* writing staff was instructed to skip dinner and get to work on some new scenes. A blood-letting hour later, we had the scenes, the director frantically restaged, the actors did some frenzied memorization, and the second taping was a smash. This only goes to prove that when you deprive writers of food, you erase the mental blocks and raise their creativity level. Just don't let this get around.

A DAY WITH GROUCHO

My most memorable rewriting experience involved one of my comedy idols. GROUCHO MARX had admitted in an interview that *Welcome Back, Kotter* was his favorite TV show. The Kotter staff was all atwitter, and plans were immediately made for Groucho to do a walk-on bit in the episode currently in production. This meant it was time for . . . REWRITES. A short scene had to be quickly inserted, and here's what we came up with:

Gabe Kotter is in the school hallway doing his Groucho impression for the Sweathogs, and, as Groucho himself passes by he says:

GROUCHO

That's the worst impression I've
ever heard.

Well, when it came time for the first taping, Groucho's nurse reported that he had gotten so excited, his blood pressure had gone up, and she couldn't allow him to go on. Groucho never appeared, but I did get to spend some quality time with a comedy legend. Groucho died a few weeks later. I think we killed him.

THE GLITCH HITCH

So, you've completed your script, the check didn't bounce, everybody thinks you're brilliant. Good for you. You've managed to avoid any of the GLITCHES that can occur during the writing process.

You HAVE avoided these glitches, haven't you?

GLITCH ONE: Quite often a writer may get "cut off" after the Story Outline has been submitted, and the First Draft assignment is given to a freelance relative or one of the show's staff writers. This could happen for a variety of reasons. The producers may think the writer didn't do the job the way they wanted. Or, the writer may be dealing with "egomaniacs" who have a compulsion to make everything their own. Believe me, these people exist. In this event, the writer is paid the 30 percent story fee, and will likely receive or share "Story By" credit.

GLITCH TWO: Your finished script (this absolute work of art that you turned in) could be completely rewritten by another writer. Go ahead and fret, but don't stew. Haul out that resilience, put your tenacity in gear, and just keep moving ahead. I strongly recommend that you always go directly on to another writing project after you have delivered your second draft because your script now belongs to the show, and you have no control over the outcome. You are no longer the owner of your own idea.

A few of my scripts have been shot completely as written; others have undergone minor rewrite surgery. But nothing tops the experience I had during one of the fallow periods of my career. I was hired to write an episode for a highly unmemorable syndicated series called *What a Country,* starring the eminent Russian humorist, Yakov Smirnoff.

I went through all the stages, got paid the full amount, and the producers told me I had turned in TV magic. When the episode aired, my script had been completely rewritten by the producers (two of those egomaniacs I've referred to). The only thing of mine that remained was one, single joke.

My poor, magic baby had been beaten senseless! Not only that, their total rewrite completely stunk and they had the audacity to keep my name on it as the writer!

Was I deeply hurt? What do you think? But I got over it quickly because I had RESILIENCE. I soldiered on because I had TENACITY.

So, if something like this ever happens to you, go ahead and get mad—experience the emotions—but don't make waves and burn bridges. It's not worth it. Just take the money and write something else. Remember, you always have your ORIGINAL script. And your agent could use that script to open another one of those doors for you.

THE CULPRIT WAS ME

While working on the staffs of various comedy shows, I have been that person who sometimes rewrote someone else's script. It was part of my job. If I thought the script had merit, I tried to retain as much of the original writer's work as possible. If the script was pretty crummy, it was my job to remove the crums.

In one curious incident, I kept the original writer's name on a total (page one) rewrite. The original writer used the script as his writing sample and he got tons of work out of it. He even wrote one of these books on how to write comedy.

Like I said, it's a nutso business.

JOINED AT THE HIP

Writing is a very lonely occupation. This is especially true in comedy because when you work alone, you don't always HEAR the laugh. This is why people often team up to write. In comedy, it's a good idea to have a "sounding board," and a big, spontaneous laugh from someone you respect is the most beautiful sound in the world.

You'll find a lot of TEAMS in the sitcom biz. They COLLABORATE for a variety of reasons. Oftentimes, one writer's weaknesses are the other writer's strengths. One may be strong in story, the other may excel at dialogue. One or the other may be better at the verbal pitch. I've known writing teams where only one is the writer, and the other the salesperson. Hey, whatever gets you there.

For six of my twenty-five–plus years as a professional writer, I have collaborated with some very talented writers, and I think it's time you met them.

GREG

When I was hired as story editor on *Love, American Style,* I had expected to work as a single. Imagine my surprise when, on the first day of work, I was introduced to my new "partner," a long-haired motorcycle rider in a black leather jacket who went by the name of GREG STRANGIS.

Greg and I were led to the office we were to share. It was a renovated broom closet with a single desk, so we took turns standing up, and the one sitting had to do the typing.

We worked long, hard hours and turned out some terrific stuff. *Love, American Style* was the perfect show for guys like us to cut our teeth on. It was like "vaudeville" for writers—a different show everyday, three shows in each weekly episode. With no regular characters or format, we were free to create whoever or whatever we wanted as long as it was built around the theme of love.

The team of Rannow & Strangis was a hit! We were HOT! We turned out over two dozen installments of *Love, American Style,* a couple of the first *Happy Days* scripts and five episodes of *Room 222,* a show that allowed us the freedom to combine comedy, drama, and social responsibility, resulting in some of our best work.

Greg credits me as the best writing teacher he ever could have had, but I was just as driven to succeed as he was, and I learned as much from Greg as he learned from me. That's the way good partnerships work.

Our collaboration lasted some three years, and Greg has since gone on to write and produce *Eight is Enough, Star Trek, Falcon Crest,* and *Jag.* About five years after our breakup, we re-united to write a very funny screenplay called *Comix.* We divided the story—each writing half the script—then we rewrote and edited each other's work. It was an interesting working arrangement that many writing teams use today. And, in case you're wondering, *Comix* never made it to the screen. It came oh-so-close, but it is now submerged in the murky waters of unsold scripts.

JEWEL

I met JEWEL JAFFE, early in my career, when we were actors in the touring company of a musical show. You get to know a person pretty well in twenty weeks on the road, and we were married six months later.

During the time I was partnered with Greg, Jewel began to develop as a writer as well. I was seeing something pretty extraordinary in her, and soon the possibility of writing with my wife became an intriguing idea.

BUT . . . I couldn't team up with my wife, I was already spoken for. Greg and I were doing fine. I agonized over this for months, then I finally followed my gut feeling and announced to Greg that I was leaving him for my wife. The breakup wasn't pleasant, but the wounds have healed.

My collaboration with Jewel began slowly. We took a year off—lived on our savings—and wrote a screenplay that also resides in motion picture limboland. That screenplay, however, attracted the attention of a very perceptive agent who immediately arranged for us to meet with the producers of a new TV comedy series called *Welcome Back, Kotter.*

The Kotter "Hotsie Totsie" story was Jewel's idea. The school she went to in New York City had a Hotsie, and, come to think of it, so did my school in Wisconsin. We developed a one-line story pitch:

"A girl named Rosalie Totsie says she's pregnant and one of the Sweathogs is the father."

That pitch immediately got us staff jobs as story editors, and our partnership was on its way.

For three amazing years, Jewel and I were on the television network "A" LIST. And even though networks deny there is such a list, being on the list was a pretty big deal, and we rode out this excellent streak until the network passed on a pilot we wrote, which had the effect of canceling our marriage.

RICH MIX

So, what did I learn from these partnerships? Glad you asked. Working with someone else in the room allowed me to think outside my own experience, and that alone made me a better writer. I will always cherish the richness of my collaborations with Greg and Jewel.

Despite my literary divorces, I have never stopped forming writing partnerships, usually on a "one project" basis because writer collaborations can often yield wonderful things, and you definitely grow in the process.

So, if you're having a hard time making it alone, think about taking on a partner. It's not for a lifetime, it can only be for a single project, but if it works, milk it for all it's worth. There's no better feeling than the exchange of humor between two funny people. It's great for the mind, eases the heart, and you'll live a lot longer.

All working TV comedy writers (whether toiling alone or in tandem) are in constant COLLABORATION with a multitude of individuals. Sitcom success depends on teamwork. It blends the talents of writers, actors, directors, and many others who lend their expertise to the final product. This being the case, it's a good idea for a new writer to be familiar with the PERSONNEL of a show, and how the writer relates to these people.

WRITERS

As a freelancer, you will inevitably find yourself creatively involved in collaborations with producers and staff writers. As a staff writer, you will often participate in highly competitive GROUP WRITING SESSIONS with everyone on the show's staff trying to come up with just the right joke to replace one that died. Whatever you do in these sessions, do not be shy or afraid. Appear fearless. Be willing to bomb. DARE TO SOUND STUPID! Your fellow writers will never hesitate to tell you your joke stinks, and when this happens, don't be thin-skinned. Just dust off your ego and rejoin the competition, so you can tell them that THEIR joke stinks.

ACTORS

Working as a freelancer, it's doubtful you will be working closely with the actors on the show. You may meet one or two of them; you may not. Depends on your luck.

As a staff writer, you're bound to see and hear a lot from the actors, so listen to them because, contrary to popular opinion, actors are people too. Avoid being impressed with their stardom; they will take care of that for you. They like you when you write them a lot of lines. They don't like you when you don't. When they corner you, and try to get you to make their part bigger or rewrite their lines, simply tell them that you'll see what you can do and, unless it makes good sense to you, don't do it. If the actor in question happens to be the star, pass the problem off to the producer, and he will deal with it by passing the problem back to you.

Here are a few significant FACTOIDS about actors:

1. Some actors are a pleasure to work with; others deserve to have their heads fitted for a dartboard.
2. Don't date the actors. Getting serious with the person your boss is in love with could lose you your job.
3. Don't expect the star of the show to say your lines as written. They like to be creative and show everyone that they could be a writer too if they weren't so busy being a star. (One star I worked with kept his own writer hidden in his dressing room. This writer was employed to write ad-libs for the actor to come up with "off the top of his head." It worked.)
4. Always be nice to the star, no matter how big an imbecile that star may be.
5. Don't make fun of the star, and don't get caught making fun of the star. They can always get another writer, but it's the star's face that the viewers tune in to see every week.

It's best if the writers and actors on the same show get along well. On one show I worked on, the writers were discouraged from hanging around with the actors, and this inane concept resulted in a pretty mediocre show. Never forget that we're all in this for only one reason—to make people laugh so hard they'll change their long distance provider.

PRODUCERS

The title "producer" sounds extremely important, and it is. I mean, you never hear of a starlet dating a writer to get ahead—it's always the producer. One of the questions I'm most frequently asked is: "What does a producer do?" Well, some do a good job and others stink up the show. Some have talent and others have connections and a knack for survival.

Most TV comedy producers are writers, which is a good thing, since—and I'm sure you will agree that this is worth repeating—WRITING is the most important element in the success of a sitcom.

The producer is the foreman (or forewoman) who runs the show. Producers hire actors, writers, directors, set designers, composers—all with the blessings or curses of the network. Strong producers reason with the network. Weak producers are run by the network.

Scripting on staff and as a freelancer, I found myself collaborating with all kinds of producers. Many of them were very good at their jobs, and it showed in the quality of the product they produced. Others were writers who, when promoted to producer, instantly reached their level of incompetence, thus proving that Peter and his Principle are alive and well in Hollywood.

I've worked for producers who were bullies and enjoyed yelling at me. One producer threw darts at me when I disagreed with him. Another was an alcoholic who became more and more dangerous as the day wore on. One producing team I worked for had no apparent personal lives, and made sure their writing staff didn't have any either. It was a seven-day-a-week job. These producers were disorganized procrastinators who made millions with a hit show.

My least favorite brand of producer is the inept variety who somehow bounce from show to show leaving a string of cancellations in their wakes. These producers survive only because, in Hollywood, it's not how good your work is, it's just good that you keep working.

DIRECTORS

Directors are revered in show business. In fact, they're so worshipped that a feature film director can become the author of a screenplay he didn't even write.

In sitcom, having your script directed by a good director can be a very rewarding experience. Talented directors are a MUST for good TV comedy, but, unfortunately, too many of these directors are simply TECHNICIANS, skilled in moving cameras, but without a clue when it comes to understanding writing. One director I worked with would constantly suggest cutting punchlines, while leaving the set-ups. He just didn't understand "funny," and it was a painful experience.

I've worked with directors who were afraid of actors because these directors didn't understand actors and acting. I recall one particular director who would actually run away and hide when confronted by an actor with a question.

The names of the wonderfully talented comedy directors are no secret. They've left their marks on such classic shows as *Cheers,* *M*A*S*H, Taxi,* and *Frasier.* But these are the cream, and once you skim off the cream there's not much left.

C'mon, Let's face facts: The best directors are, and always will be, those who have been writers and/or actors. So, the field is wide open. There's a desperate need. And a wise writer, who has an affinity for people, should seriously look into directing. It will give you a lot more control over your own writing.

THE GLUE PEOPLE

The population of a sitcom includes many SECRETARIES and PRODUCTION ASSISTANTS: They are the glue that holds the show together. All writers (both freelance and staff) should make it a point to be nice to these valuable individuals. They are your collaborators, not your underlings. I've seen many people in these positions go on to be producers and development executives. And, believe me, they always remember how they were treated and by who, whom, whatever.

IT'S ALL RELATIVE

In show business, you will often notice a lot of people with similar last names. These are card-carrying relatives of someone important. Treat these people with respect. If you don't they will rat on you. NEPOTISM is a grand show business tradition, which has led many a sitcom into cancellation.

COLLABORATION ABERRATION

Successful collaborations are essential in the sitcom world . . . BUT. "But what," you ask with trepidation. "But," I answer, "it's a business filled with extremely diverse personalities, many of whom are intent on—or just haplessly responsible for—screwing up."

Sometimes the screwing up is UNINTENTIONAL. A good example is a show I worked on called *Sweepstakes.* The original concept of *Sweepstakes* was a one-hour comedy/drama format, with three overlapping stories. Each week we would show a different person win a tax-free million dollars from the state lottery. (A measly million? That's all? Must have been a studio budgetary decision.)

Every episode concerned the lives of three of the finalists and how the money they won—either the $1 million or the $1,000 runner-up prize—affected their lives. The "lottery" concept had been knocking around for quite a few years, and it was finally being given a chance.

The producer of *Sweepstakes* hired me as his story editor, and we clicked immediately. We felt our collaboration was turning out great scripts, and were finally going to make this concept work by making this concept funny.

Unfortunately, the network and studio executives did not share our enthusiasm or our vision. Their collaborative efforts amounted to constant "tampering." There was a pervasive fear among these executives based on their limited knowledge or distrust of comedy. They had no clear vision of what the show was about because, according to their executive memos, it was about something different on a daily basis.

A decision was finally made to chuck funny altogether and make the show strictly dramatic fare. I was let go and they hired a writer to "punch down" all my comedy stories. *Sweepstakes* ran on NBC for two months before it was canceled—an unfortunate casualty of a collaboration that lacked collaborators.

All writers must keep a close watch on the tinkering that is done with most TV comedy scripts. As an episodic scribe, you'll get network notes, studio notes, and notes from the show's staff writers. This is where you have to be confident that you know the material best, while at the same time having the smarts to adapt to a better idea when you see one. It's a rough, literary terrain, full of verbal land mines that distort and destroy. So be very careful of the direction others want you to take.

Incidents of toxic collaboration can also result when dealing with cunning types who are INTENTIONALLY bent on screwing up. This can occur when a writer shows signs of weakness or uncertainty. I once had an agent who took strange advantage of our professional collaboration at a low point in my career.

Now, a writer expects an agent to display loyalty and negotiate the best possible deal, but that's not always the case. I had been offered a six-month job as head writer on a sitcom being shot in Canada. The idea of heading north to work in a different country intrigued me, so what kind of deal were they offering?

My agent projected agonizing frustration: Oh, woe, as hard as he had tried, he couldn't get them to pay what I usually got. Not only that, they couldn't pay per diem, so (except for air fare) I'd have to pay my own expenses. It was a lousy, creepy deal, but nothing else was happening for me, so I took it.

Later, I found out the producer/creator of the Canadian show was also my loyal agent's client. I felt used. I had been the pawn in a lousy, creepy game devised to save money.

Too many people in show business function in mysterious ways, so learn from my mistakes and keep a cautious eye out for these sly devils. Always remain on your best behavior when dealing with people who screw you. Don't blow up or make a scene, and NEVER set out to get even. Kill them with class. Your continuing success after they are history will be revenge enough.

Comedy has a rule of three, and apparently so does the process of screwing up. As you've seen, there's unintentional, intentional, and number three, POLITICAL.

I was only on the staff of *Welcome Back, Kotter* for the first two seasons, and what I am about to relate happened during seasons three and four, but a lot of friends on the show kept me informed, so here's what took place . . .

Gabe Kaplan played Kotter and Kotter was supposed to be the star, but John Travolta had exploded into stardom, and the show could have been retitled *Welcome Back, Barbarino*. Travolta's character had caught on big with the TV audience. And a lot of it had to do with jokes like this one from a *Kotter* episode I wrote with Jewel, called "Follow the Leader, Parts 1 & 2." In this scene, Gabe's wife, Julie, has walked out on him because he is spending so much time with his students.

> GABE
>
> Vinnie, she left me . . .
>
> BARBARINO
>
> Mr. Kotter, don't worry. It's
> just like the time Mimsy Mendolia
> walked out on me. I knew it was
> just a matter of time before she'd come
> runnin' back.
>
> GABE
>
> She came running back?
>
> BARBARINO
>
> No, but it's just a matter of time.

The audience loved Barbarino. Kaplan was very unhappy about Travolta's stunning popularity, and his dissatisfaction spread, causing nonfiction friction throughout Kotter's real world.

Soon, with Travolta becoming a movie star and making only infrequent appearances on the show, the ratings began to sag, igniting a power struggle between Kaplan and executive producer, Jimmy Komack. This feud reached a peak when a group of people loyal to Kaplan (writers, directors) were fired, and the producer/writer team from *The Carol Burnett Show* was brought in to replace them.

These people had written sensational *Carol Burnett Shows,* but their *Kotter* episodes sucked. The result was that Kaplan walked out on the show. He only appeared in a few episodes during the final season. Politics ruined *Welcome Back, Kotter,* and what had been destined to be at least a five-year show, barely limped through its fourth season.

THE DARK SIDE OF SUCCESS

I've read more than one interview in which a successful writer says that he writes for the creative satisfaction, NOT for the money. Don't you believe it. Hollywood writers DO derive a great deal of creative jollies from what they do, but the amounts of money you can earn are astounding, and that sort of lure can become addictive. In fact, the basic code of law in Hollywood is that money equals success, and success is all that matters.

You can probably tell where I'm going with this. I'm about to give you some advice on dealing with the MONEY and the SUCCESS that is well within your grasp.

THE DAY OF THE PREDATORS

The reading of the first *Welcome Back, Kotter* script was held inside a cavernous soundstage at NBC in Burbank. *Kotter* was an ABC show, so why it was being shot at NBC is anybody's guess.

Kotter had yet to hit the air, but the word was already out that it would be a hit, so this gathering was a prime opportunity for what I call THE DAY OF THE PREDATORS.

They came from everywhere seeking prey (I mean, clients). They were agents, personal managers, business managers, real estate people, lawyers—all getting chummy with the writers, actors, and others soon to be making big money being funny.

The real comedy here is that most of us were taken in by this mating ritual, which I was told is an old Hollywood tradition.

Jewel and I were about to make some very hefty cash when this ritual began, and we fell for it. Those present began to romance us, knowing full well that we were about to make boo-koo commissionable bucks, plus residuals.

(The lowdown on Residuals coming up soon. Stay tuned.)

I recall one particular meeting that Jewel and I attended shortly after we left the staff of *Kotter,* a meeting to solidify our ABC and Columbia Studio development deals. As the two of us gazed around the room, reality finally hit us. We had an agent, a personal manager, a business manager, and a lot of other people in the room, who we were suddenly responsible for making rich. At least 30 percent of what we hadn't made yet was already in somebody else's pocket. Only our real estate agent wasn't at the meeting. She was in Mexico spending the commission she had just raked in from selling us our big Spanish house in Beverly Hills with a parrot and a pool the size of Cleveland.

All of this fame and fortune lasted about a year and a half, until Jewel and I dissolved our marriage, our partnership, and our corporation. We offered our associates 30 percent of our split, but suddenly no takers.

In retrospect, I now realize that I was giving away my life to others. I was too busy being an "artist," and couldn't be bothered with the mundane things in life like paying bills. I was so taken in by money and success that it never occurred to me that the only people Jewel and I REALLY needed in our lives were our agent, an accountant to do our taxes, and a live-in marriage counselor.

So, learn from my mistakes, and keep one important thing in mind: Elvis needed a personal manager; TV comedy writers DON'T need a personal manager. Ted Turner needs a business manager to handle his money and pay his bills, but NOT you. Pay your own bills. Always know where your money is, and keep a close eye on where your money is going, because somewhere I lost track, and suddenly the money was gone.

Pitfalls of this sort happen to too many writers. It led me to individual therapy, group therapy, massage therapy, Rolfing, and Buddhism.

But there was yet another pitfall. The biggest of all. A real doozy.

UP YOUR NOSE

The most dangerous predators present on *Kotter's* opening day were the COKE dealers. (Not the beverage, the therapy taken by nose.) Cocaine dealers are drawn to Hollywood because that's where the big money is. I didn't know who these people were at first, but it didn't take me long to find out.

Freddie Prinze was starring in *Chico & the Man,* a comedy series that was being shot on the stage next to ours. I walked into an office one day and discovered Freddie and a fellow writer friend snorting white lines of powder. I said, "What's that stuff?" which met with major laughter because they thought I had cracked a great joke, but I wasn't joking. I was serious.

I really didn't know what that stuff was that was turning their noses white. I was a very straight kid from the Midwest who thought that drugs were not to be tolerated. If someone was smoking marijuana at a party, I would leave the party. I was a straight and narrow hard-liner . . . until that day.

Freddie asked me to join in, and I went for it. I was with a big star, and didn't want to appear "unhip." I mean, if he was doing it, how bad could it be?

It wasn't bad at all. It furnished a euphoria that seemed to lend itself well to the pressures and long hours on the job. I soon bought some of my own. And then some more. And some more . . .

SNOW IN L.A.

Many of the TV comedy series of the 1970s were written on cocaine. All of Hollywood was supposedly doing it. People were wearing coke spoons and razor blades on gold chains around their necks. There were rumors that some show-business executives were actually supplying coke for the talent they were working with.

Coke was included in budgets. Contracts contained cleverly disguised drug clauses that provided the drug as part of the deal. My favorite rumor was that Redd Foxx *(Sanford & Sons)* had the inside of his nose replaced with a kind of aluminum siding. But it was only a rumor.

There was soon an epidemic of "sinus conditions" on the Hollywood scene. "Sniff, sniff . . . Man, this smog is killing me." Hey, it was new, it was cool, it was exotic, it was expensive. A drug dealer moved right next door to me, so I had handy access. I think this was the beginning of the Home Shopping Network.

Did the coke make me a better writer? Oh, I thought so at first, but all it did was make me unsatisfyingly driven, and a real hoot at parties. There was no reality anymore, just Hollywood. And the friendly coke dealer next door. I can only hope he invested my money wisely, but he most likely stuffed it up his own nose.

FREDDIE

Freddie Prinze changed it all when he died from putting a gun to his head. He had been on a steady diet of coke (an upper) and Quaaludes (a downer), and I guess his body gave up trying to decide. Freddie was only twenty-two years old, the funniest and most polished comedian I had ever seen.

The day Freddie died, a whole lot of Hollywood types took a good look at what they were doing. Maybe they were inhaling a fast finish to their own futures. So, at the present time, I suspect there has been a significant reduction in Hollywood's romance with cocaine and other drugs that lead to failure. At least I certainly hope so.

I don't do coke anymore. I found out I can create without that stuff, so why pay the money and go through the hassle? People take drugs because they need a crutch, and that crutch soon begets a drug dealer moving in next door.

Okay, so what am I saying? What I am saying is that if somebody offers you a white line of powder, take it as an opportunity to sneeze. It's a great way to keep your nose clean.

SOLIDARITY

Okay, big shot, you've done it! It's official. You've overcome all the baggage that comes with the process of selling an idea and putting your life on loan to a sitcom. You've imagined, you've crafted, you've delivered. The checks really were in the mail. You have just won an $18,000 lottery, plus residuals, if the show you wrote for produces enough total episodes to make syndicated and/or cable reruns financially feasible.

(More about residuals momentarily—a fascinating phenomenon.)

As of the writing of this book, the WRITERS' GUILD OF AMERICA's Minimum Basic Agreement stipulates that the fees for half-hour scripts are paid in three installments of the $17,940.00 total:

1. STORY—30%
2. FIRST DRAFT—40%
3. FINAL DRAFT—The balance of the total.

That's a lot of funny money, isn't it? Why, a person could buy three or four beanie babies at auction with that kind of dough. Yeah, TV writers are well paid, that's for sure. But this did not come about by accident.

The idea of writers having a union began to take shape back in 1933 when studio executives wanted to cut everyone's salary but their own by 50 percent to "save the industry."

Finally angered by these constant attempts at creative hijacking, a small group of gutsy writers got together, despite threats to end their careers, and took on the likes of such motion picture luminaries as Louis B. ("You'll never work in this town again") Mayer and Jack L. ("There's no blacklist, I do it by phone") Warner. Three separate Guilds—the Radio Writers, the TV Writers, and the Screen Writers—all joined together, and in 1954, the Writers' Guild of America (WGA) was born.

UNION BLUES

When I sold my first script, I began to qualify for membership in the WGA, an organization you must belong to if you want to get a job, but can't belong to unless you have a job.

Qualification is based on a point system—various stages of scriptwriting are worth a certain amount of points. If you write an entire thirty-minute story and teleplay, you're halfway there. (For more on this, see Appendix B.)

Now, I have to admit that my personal experience being admitted as a union member was cloaked in some initial bitterness. I had finally gotten my long-sought-after break, even better yet, a STAFF job! So, imagine my chagrin when the day after I received my coveted WGA membership card, the Guild went out on STRIKE.

Thus began many a rainy morning parading back and forth in front of Warner Brothers Studio. These early morning forays were important in helping me develop a mature attitude toward my profession as I marched shoulder-to-shoulder with writers who never hesitated to share their views with me:

EXT. WARNER BROTHERS STUDIO - EARLY MORNING

IT'S THE RAINY SEASON IN L.A. A REAL DOWNPOUR. TORRENTS OF
WATER SURGE DOWN THE STREET CARRYING CHUNKS OF MALIBU INTO
THE SAN FERNANDO VALLEY. NOT A SOUL IN SIGHT EXCEPT FOR
<u>JERRY</u> AND AN INTENSE-LOOKING <u>FELLOW WRITER</u>. THEY SHARE A
SMALL UMBRELLA AND HOLD PICKET SIGNS—"NO REPLACEMENT
WRITERS!"—"LET THE DIRECTORS WRITE THE SCRIPTS." THE STRIKE
IS GOING INTO ITS THIRD MONTH.

                    JERRY

        (TO FELLOW WRITER) I hear the
        studios are about to settle.

               FELLOW WRITER

        Settle?? We blow up their cars,
        rip off their heads and suck out
        their guts! THAT'S how you settle!

Pearls of wisdom from a seasoned pro. This man has written a string
of hit action flicks. You may be one of the billions who've seen
them.

Many months and two and a half pairs of sneakers later, the
union and the studios reached a settlement, the strike was finally over,
and the union held a meeting to tell us that we'd achieve our REAL
goals during the next strike.

Was I angry? You bet I was. Uncommonly pissed is a good
way to describe my actual feeling at the time. Why couldn't the union
have had their stupid strike the year before, when I was still a nobody?
What the hell does a writer need a union for anyway?

It wasn't long before I found out why. The more I became
exposed to the Guild and its purposes, the more I realized that if
it wasn't for this show of solidarity, writers would be working for next
to nothing, excluding residuals. When that small, gutsy group of writers banded together, there were no contracts, no minimums, no pension or health protection—writers had no control over their own
existence, and were expected to live off either the land or their rich
Uncle Floyd.

Through the years, the Guild has engaged in many battles with management and, today, the WGA stands strongly for the basic rights and the professional identity of all writers. For dues of $25 or 1.5 percent of your total earnings each quarter, it's a real bargain.

FOUND MONEY

Which brings us to RESIDUALS! Yes, it's that inspirational, fascinating, riveting phenomenon I have been promising to tell you all about. Residuals are a blessing for anyone who writes for television, and you are about to see why.

When you write a sitcom script, and are paid the Writers' Guild minimum, the union sees to it that you continue to get paid if the episode you wrote is repeated. You will receive a percentage of the original scriptwriting fee. The current residual formula—as of this writing—is as follows:

2nd RUN—50% if on ABC, CBS, or NBC / 55% if on FOX
3rd RUN—40% if on ABC, CBS, or NBC / 41.25% if on FOX.
4th to 6th RUN—25% for each run / 34.375% if on FOX.
7th to 10th RUN—15% for each run / 20.625% if on FOX.
11th & 12th RUN—10% for each run / 13.750% if on FOX.
13th RUN & each run thereafter—5% / 6.875% if on FOX.

For basic cable and syndication, the WGA's residual formula is based on the "producer's (owner's) gross," or the total amount a producer earns on the repeated runs of a sitcom. Writers receive 1.5 percent of the producer's gross for the first million dollars earned and 1.8 percent of every dollar earned above 1 million.

So, what is the producer's gross? How do you know what it is? Forget it; you could take entirely too much time trying to find this out for yourself (OR) you could leave it to the WGA's experienced staff who are experts in the field, monitoring and enforcing payments from all over the world on the writer's behalf.

The Writers' Guild is very diligent about tracking down what is owed to writers. It collects the money and forwards the checks to you. It even administers the collection and distribution of FOREIGN RESIDUALS that are owed to writers. I recently received a $1.35 residual for a *Happy Days* episode that was aired in France. I blew it all on french fries at McDonald's.

I've made a lot of money on residuals during my career, and it's always a delight to find that envelope marked RESIDUAL in the mailbox. During "valley" periods, those unexpected checks are especially welcome. When you figure that you've earned around $18,000 for your original episode, you're still garnering roughly $900 or so for a tenth run.

These residual formulas were not given to the Writers' Guild; they were wrenched out of management's pockets. As I've already illustrated, there were long strikes in which writers walked the picket lines for months to get some kind of proper monetary recognition for their creative efforts. These Guild members fought hard to get these formulas, and they are constantly being improved.

Personally, I've been through three strikes at a substantial loss of income. No, I didn't like it, but the strikes always resulted in significant gains for all television writers in today's expanding markets. And you, the writers of the future, will reap these gains. I hope you're grateful, you lucky stiffs.

WRITER-FRIENDLY

Today, various Guild Departments provide services to writers in such areas as membership, agencies, residuals, and pension and health. They've got it all pretty well covered.

The WGA publishes a membership directory, and conducts seminars, workshops, and conferences. The award-winning *Written By* is the monthly magazine of the WGA. Nonmembers can subscribe by calling (323) 782-4522 or by sending an e-mail to *writtenby@wga.org*.

It should be noted that the Guild's Board of Directors has established a "contract adjustment" committee to negotiate with management on a constant basis in order to avoid strikes, which are damaging to both sides. This new approach to labor relations has resulted in steady improvement and upgrades in the Guild's MINIMUM BASIC AGREEMENT (MBA).

I find the MBA an entrancing document. There's nothing I relish more than an open fire on a nippy evening—a hot cup of nog in one hand, a copy of the MBA in the other. Ah, what a pleasant way to pass an evening. Hey, I may joke, but the MBA is serious stuff—wrought through the continuing efforts of fellow Guild members and staff. Recently, a contract was won to protect writers in the field of animation, which means that writer/actor Daffy Duck is now a Guild member and plans to run for the Board of Directors.

There's a media revolution going on out there, and as it continues its incredibly influential growth, the Writers' Guild of America will be viligant in its initiation and protection of all writers' economic and creative rights.

For more information on the WRITERS' GUILD OF AMER-ICA, you have three choices:

1. Call the Guild's Los Angeles office at: (323) 951-4000.
2. Visit the Guild's Web site: *www.wga.org*
3. Turn to APPENDIX C at the back of this book.

PILOT DREAMS

I woke up in a cold sweat the other night. I think it was my sleep-in muse's way of reminding me that this book should probably address the subject of PILOTS. You know what pilots are: They're one-episode samples of a projected TV comedy series created by you that you hope will run for twenty years or until it shows a profit, whichever comes first.

I think I've stated pretty clearly by now that the only entree into the realm of sitcom is that "spec" script of a current show. That's what all the talk has been about up until this point, so if the message hasn't sunk in, go back, start over, and this time pay attention, okay?

Until recently, there was no such thing as a "spec" pilot script from a new writer because network and studio executives had no frame of reference when dealing with characters they were unfamiliar with.

Not so anymore. Today, many in the industry will be happy for your agent to submit a pilot script with original characters created by you. If you tell a good story, show an exceptional sense of humor, and write funny characters who jump into the reader's lap, you'll likely get that phone call you've been hoping for.

Forget about receiving a call from a network executive begging you to do a pilot. This is a major investment for them, so it ain't gonna happen. Networks only commission pilots from writers with a proven track record.

If you've written a pilot, by all means show it—but consider it a SALES TOOL that may open one of those doors for you. Your sales tool may even be placed into the hands of an already successful TV creator (called a "show runner"), and where this person runs with your show is up for grabs, but it could be the beginning of a successful collaboration; there's nothing like starting out right at the top.

ACCORDING TO THE BIBLE

Developing a pilot requires a great deal of finite thought: Focus on character, a compelling story idea, and the ability to express your idea in one line, which is called a "log line." For example, the classic *Mary Tyler Moore Show* could be described this way: A show about a young career woman, and how she balances her job with her personal life. Simple. No details. That's the whole nut in a shell.

I believe it is necessary to write out a six- or seven-page BIBLE, which tells the reader what the show is about. Your Bible should tell the reader where the show takes place, who the main character is, and what that character is like. The reader will also want to know who the other regulars are who interact with your main character. Your characters, and their relationships with each other, must come to life on the page.

Your Bible must provide the reader with a brief synopsis of the pilot story, as well as short paragraphs on three or four other stories that establish a direction for the series. Then, having done all of this, commit your entire Bible to memory because you'll probably be expected to pitch it verbally.

Then, when someone buys your pilot pitch, they'll want to see it in writing—and you'll already have it in writing because you've already written it! See how neatly that works out? News of a sale will, of course, thrill your agent who can now commence doing the agent thing and carve out a huge deal for your future.

I have so many of these thirty-minute pilot Bibles in my office, I could rent out the place for half-hour prayer meetings. A few of my pilot ideas have crashed on takeoff; some actually became airborne, but ran out of gas. I got paid option money on a number of them—and received huge script payments on a total of seven—all of which were sucked into the Network Triangle and never heard from again.

RARIFIED AIR

Okay, let's say you've broken the barrier—you've accomplished something quite unusual: You got somebody to read your spec pilot. That somebody liked it and passed it on to the aforementioned show runner. The show runner liked it, ran it by the network, and it SOLD!

Good goin', babe! Fees for pilots vary anywhere from $25,000 to hundreds of thousands of dollars, depending on the writer's clout and the ability of the writer's agent to make the writer an overnight rich person.

A word of caution, however. This is not a good time to change your hairstyle, your spouse, or your friends because they don't measure up to your genius. No, don't do that. Just pause for a moment, give thanks, and take a look at these PILOT POINTERS you should be aware of:

1. Many network executives lack a sense of humor. But for some reason these people always seem to be put in charge of developing comedy shows. They don't always know what's funny or why it's funny, and when they ask you to start explaining each joke, pop a dramamine and get ready for an unforgettable voyage.

2. Network executives have a constant hunger for a big hit, so they're depending on you to deliver. That's why they're paying you an obscene amount of their department's money for your half-hour pilot script.

3. If you are lucky enough to land on the network schedule, you'll have roughly one or two episodes to prove that you can draw an audience. The days of a thirteen-episode guarantee are history, unless Monica Lewinsky is attached to star.

4. If your show is put on the air, it will only be as good as its TIME SLOT. A show will never be a hit without a good time slot. (*Wings* followed *Cheers*. *Suddenly Susan* followed *Seinfeld*.) It's a case of a healthy mother giving birth to an ailing child, who despite the affliction, grows up to be an annoying adult.

5. Network executives are insecure people. It comes with the job. They are under extreme pressure to deliver shows that will sell FORDS, MCI, and TACO BELL.

6. Developing a pilot script with network executives is tantamount to forecasting the weather. There's usually a disturbance somewhere, and if nothing seems to be going wrong, there are more than enough people around to make sure that there will be.

7. Network executives usually have a MARKETING background, so treat them to "toys" like charts, graphs, and crystal balls.

8. Network executives are usually scheduled to be fired from their jobs at any moment, but treat them with respect because tomorrow they may fail upward.

9. To paraphrase screenwriter William Goldman: No one in show business knows anything! This is especially true of TV. Success is a process in which all those concerned— writers, producers, studio big shots, network executives—take their best and worst guesses and stumble them blindly through (good or bad) luck.

10. Networks used to set trends; now they follow them. You will be asked to take whatever is hot at the moment and repeat it. FEAR runs wild in the TV business, and when creativity is stifled, a weak or careless writer will often pay the price. Always remember that TV is in a continual state of change, so be a part of that change. Commit to and defend your own, ORIGINAL concepts. The future is you.

And, finally, and most important . . .

11. Defend your vision. When it comes to the script you wrote, no one knows more about it than YOU—the WRITER.

I hope these Pilot Pointers are of help to you as you go through the process of putting your own pilot on the air. May Shecky, the god of comedy, shower you with funny money.

LAGNIAPPE

LAGNIAPPE (pronounced "Lan-Yap") was the name of the column I wrote for my school newspaper at the University of Wisconsin–Milwaukee (where *Happy Days'* Richie Cunningham also went to school). Lagniappe is a seldom-used word that means "to give more," so this chapter will provide you with insights into some of the little things you should be aware of if you want to write TV comedy for a living.

BED DOWN IN L.A.

If you seriously intend to become an active toiler in sitcomland, you can't do it from Sheboygan Falls. You MUST live (or at least have a place to crash) in Los Angeles.

L.A. is not the easiest city to live in. People say that it's a phoney, back-stabbing, money-grubbing place, but that's only a vicious rumor started by the people who live there. The fact is, there are just too many people. And very few of these people are actually from L.A. They move out from the East and they're always moaning that they miss the four seasons. I don't understand all this moaning. L.A. has FIVE seasons—fire, flood, mudslide, earthquake, and Academy Awards. So, with all this excitement, what is there to complain about?

THE COMPETITION WON'T KILL YOU

As you may have figured out by now, a career as a major wit is no easy task. The sitcom field is enormously competitive, with thousands moving to L.A. every year in search of the comedy grail. Whatever you do, don't let this discourage you. Most of these people probably don't come close to matching your talent, but (with thousands of spec scripts out there) they do cause major clutter and slow down the marketing machinery. Because of this unfortunate reality, experience in bartending and waiting tables, plus incredible patience, are imperative for any aspiring writer. Maintain that hope. Keep writing. That one in a million is YOU.

WEAVE A WEB

It's important to NETWORK with people in television as much as possible. Make contacts and keep in regular touch. Establish relationships. In those "valley" periods of a career, a writer depends on friends.

ITSY BITSY CREDITS

Just a few words about CREDITS. Specifically, the credits at the END of a sitcom. What happened to them? If you're lucky enough to have your credit at the beginning of a show, people will likely see your name. But if your credit appears at the end of a show, your name whips past us in a small box in the upper corner of the screen, while the network promotes the show coming on next. In many cases, this could be the network's form of apology for what the viewers just had to sit through.

TITLES

As an aspiring writer, you've probably noticed some rather confusing TITLES in the credits of a sitcom. Titles like "Executive Script Consultant," "Executive Story Consultant," "Supervising Producer,"

"Story Editor," and "Executive Story Editor." These titles—as varied and impressive as they sound—all mean only one thing: WRITER. It's just a matter of your agent negotiating a fancy, schmancy title. Heck, we'd probably call ourselves "Emperor," "Grand Wazir," and "Imperial Poobah" if the Writers' Guild allowed it.

LAUGHTRACKS

No book about TV comedy should go without a mention of LAUGH-TRACKS. The majority of sitcoms today shoot before a live audience in order to get real, spontaneous laughter.

An actress friend of mine hires herself out as a professional laugher. She's got the kind of laugh that's contagious and gets other people to break up. Any smart producer wants her at the taping of his pilot.

When there's no professional laugher at work, a writer can only pray for real laughs and, if there are no laughs, the show is forcibly "sweetened" with canned laughter.

Years ago, I met the man who provides this laughter. He carries around a small recorder box that can deliver snickers, guffaws, titters, chortles, belly laughs, horse laughs, you name it. I asked him where he got these laughs, and he told me they were from old *I Love Lucy* shows. So, the next time you hear an audience burst into raucous laughter on an episode of *Saved By the Bell,* chances are good that those people are really laughing at Lucy.

COMEDY MOVIES OF THE WEEK?

As of this writing, the networks haven't produced a comedy Movie of the Week in years. Nothing to make us feel good or bring joy to our hearts. So, what's their problem? Is it that they don't think a comedy writer is capable of being funny for two hours? No, I doubt it. I think the real reason is that the network executives don't understand comedy. It's not taught at the Harvard Business School; therefore, these individuals are afraid of it. They can't control it, and they fear anything they can't control. As a result, we're being fed a steady diet of cornball dramas about battered women in jeopardy as they fight a rare disease while having their children stolen by a mentally deranged husband intent on blowing up the world. All based on a true story. This repetitive goulash is repeated weekly, which, when you think of it, is pretty funny in itself. Help! Comedy police!

FEATURE FILMS

They're nice to write. You can do it at home, and never have to talk to a TV executive. Trouble is, you have to talk to a movie executive. Some writers have gotten millions for a single script. Even a screenplay that doesn't sell can be a great entree into show business, but it's an ENTIRELY DIFFERENT BUSINESS from TV comedy, with a whole new cast of players, so I don't advise using a screenplay as a TV sample.

OH, CANADA

Thanks to a four-letter word spelled v-i-s-a, I have had opportunities to work on two Canadian sitcoms—one in Toronto, one in Montreal. Canadian sitcoms are just as good as most American versions, but we seldom get to see them. It must be the language difference. I enjoyed very much working with the Canadians, and there are a lot of good writers up there. The only problem is, once a Canadian writer gets work, he immediately crashes Hollywood where he can easily impersonate an American and get paid more.

One interesting sidebar of my Canadian experience was meeting hockey great Wayne Gretzky, who was guesting on an episode I had written. Wayne's a super guy, and I got to spend a couple of days working closely with him, teaching him how to act. It didn't work. Later, Wayne wisely married an actress and he now lives in the United States where he is impersonating an American.

MY LUNCH
WITH ERIC

In the old days of vaudeville, the most impressive act went on "next to closing." In keeping with that honored show business tradition, this chapter is devoted to an interview with TV comedy writer, ERIC COHEN. Eric has amazing experience in the field, and is what I would refer to as a "pro's pro." His many credits include stints on *The Tonight Show*, *Welcome Back, Kotter* (co-creator), *Laverne & Shirley*, *The Golden Girls*, and, most recently, *The Nanny* and *Everybody Loves Raymond*. Eric has provided laughs for the nation on a very regular basis.

My lunch with Eric took place at Jerry's Deli (no relation) in Studio City, California:

Jerry: Eric, I'm going to ask you some questions about comedy writing, so think of this as a funny lunch.

Eric: Only if someone else is paying.

(THE WAITRESS APPEARS, WE ORDER, THEN DOWN TO BUSINESS.)

Jerry: How did you get started in comedy?

Eric: I was Mr. Funny Pants in grammar school.

Jerry: What were some of the bits you pulled?

Eric: I remember the first time I was kicked out of school. Actually, it was junior high school in Levittown, New York.

Jerry: That's that place on Long Island where they built all those look-alike houses?

Eric: They just added water, stirred, and houses appeared. Anyway, I was in the advanced class and we subscribed to the *New York Times*—which was very chic in the eighth grade—and there was this article about the proliferation of mental illness among public school teachers, and in the other section of the paper, there happened to be a new gorilla at the Bronx Zoo. So, I cut them both out, put them together on the bulletin board in front of the room, and when the teacher walked in and saw them, he said: "Cohen, get out!"

Jerry: Did this happen to you often?

Eric: It was typical of junior high school. In high school, we moved to California, where I was editor of my school newspaper and started writing a humor column. That carried over to USC, where I started a satire magazine. The name of my column was "Mein Kampus."

Jerry: I'll bet that went over big.

Eric: Hey, O. J. Simpson and I were the most popular undergrads at that time.

Jerry: You got some good press for some of the things you did, right?

Eric: Yeah, at USC, there was an election for student body president and I ran for "Military Strongman." I said basically that I was going to nationalize the schools. The *L.A. Times* did a front page story, noting that I was the first politician in American history to endorse pollution.

Jerry: Why would you do that?

Eric: I was hoping to get contributions from Union Oil.

Jerry: Makes sense to me.

Eric: Also, during this time, I started to do some of my material in the form of stand-up at a place called The Icehouse in

Pasadena, and every Saturday night, just before I was ready to go on, somebody like George Carlin or Lily Tomlin would come in unannounced to break in their new material. So, that's who I ended up following.

Jerry: Didn't go well, huh?

Eric: Actually, it went okay. I was getting a lot of attention and good reviews, but I was slowly being drawn toward writing because people would see my stand-up and then hire me to write stuff. That's how I met Gabe Kaplan.

Jerry: Gabe was doing stand-up then?

Eric: Yeah, he was an up-and-coming comic and looking for material, so I started selling him jokes, including parts of my act, much of what ultimately became part of *Welcome Back, Kotter*. And, simultaneously to this, Johnny Carson and *The Tonight Show* moved from New York to Los Angeles and they were looking for writers.

Jerry: How did they find you?

Eric: I submitted material. By then I had an agent, but I was ready. I mean, I don't believe you create a break, but you, in a way, prepare yourself your entire life, so that when opportunity comes, you're poised to seize it.

Jerry: A true nugget of wisdom.

Eric: You bet, because I didn't have to sit down and write the material I submitted to Carson . . . I went through my files, because by then I had accumulated a lot of jokes.

Jerry: So, you handed in a series of jokes?

Eric: A monologue. You wake up in the morning, open up the newspaper, and draw upon the events of the day . . . And it became the best first job for a comedy writer because my tenure writing for Carson was coincidental with Richard Nixon and Watergate . . . Nixon was just the best comic target.

Jerry: Yeah, he should've shaved closer . . . Okay, I wanna move on here . . . Let's go back to when you were a child. Were you encouraged to be funny?

Eric: Sure, absolutely.

Jerry: Your parents . . . they saw something there?

Eric: It was a household in which humor and wit were prized.

Jerry:	Your mom and dad were both funny?
Eric:	Often at my expense . . . The way I opened my act was, while I am Jewish, my parents were not. They raised me as a Jew so there would be a minority group within the family to discriminate against.
Jerry:	Do you remember your very first joke?
Eric:	It was probably something about breaking wind.
Jerry:	Breaking wind always got a laugh.
Eric:	Yeah, those were the days.
Jerry:	Give me your favorite joke.
Eric:	Well, I don't actually have a favorite . . . Let's see . . . One time I talked about growing up in a tough neighborhood, and the gangs couldn't afford guns, so they had to insert the bullets manually.
Jerry:	That was your joke?
Eric:	That was my joke. I've had people steal it and pitch it back to me.
Jerry:	Did you study writing in school?
Eric:	In a way . . . I'd work on the newspaper . . . I would always turn a school assignment into something comic. I always wrote, always had some avenue of expression.
Jerry:	And that would get you good grades?
Eric:	Well, it got me attention. Everybody knew I wasn't able to follow a straight line from Point A to Point B, and that's what comedy is—to surprise people—to get laughs from something hopefully unexpected.
Jerry:	You think you can teach someone to be funny?
Eric:	It's a sense.
Jerry:	So, you have to be born with it?
Eric:	Well, a sense of humor is one of those things that every person thinks they have . . . I mean, everybody hasn't shared the experience of performing eye surgery, but everybody has shared the experience of being funny at some point in his life, so we all have access to that experience . . . The difference is, when you do this professionally, you have to do it regularly and on demand. And that's the hard part. The fastest way to shut somebody up at a party is to tell them to be funny.

Jerry: Do you spend a lot of time writing?

Eric: I try to spend as little time writing as possible. My method is as follows: When I'm writing a script, I don't lock into time so much as I do pages. I have a kind of a daily goal for myself, and I try to write five, six, seven pages a day, and the sooner I get them done, the sooner I stop. Some days are obviously better than others and I, by far, have the best success in the morning.

Jerry: Where do you find your stories?

Eric: The longer I do this, the more obvious it is that you have to look within. The best stuff is always taken from the pages of your life. Once, Carl Reiner was talking about *The Dick Van Dyke Show,* which was about his life at the time, and he said something like: "What piece of earth do I stand on alone?" . . . I could give you a specific example of mine that I turned into an episode . . .

Jerry: Sure, go with it.

Eric: When I was on the staff of *The Nanny,* I wrote an episode based on the following incident: When one of my kids was in the first grade, we had a parents' meeting at school, and we asked permission to allow our children to participate in a kind of "adopt a grandmother" program—the idea being that once a week all the kids would go to a rest home, find an old lady, and be nice to her and have cookies. The kid would get to bond with an old person, and the old person would obviously benefit from the attention. So, we did this for a while until a mother came in and said: "Heather is not going to participate in this! This program is horrible!" . . . We asked her what the problem was, and she said: "She's lost three grandmothers this semester. She can't take it anymore!"

Jerry: So, you ran home and started taking notes?

Eric: Yes. I wrote an episode called "The Curse of the Grandmas," where Fran is a Brownie leader, and every time her little charge gets assigned to a grandmother, the woman promptly drops dead, and the kid is now considered a jinx. Whenever the kid walks into the room, these old women get on their walkers and in their chairs and take off.

Jerry: How do you organize these thoughts? Do you use an out-line?

Eric: I do copious outlining. People have always commented that my outlines are almost first drafts. You have to do the work sooner or later, so I write ten to twelve pages, single-spaced, with some dialogue, and if the outline is good, my first draft is my second draft.

Jerry: Do you believe in inspiration?

Eric: Well, I think it's indefinable; a lot of it is accumulated wisdom. I think it was Ray Bradbury who said: "Inspiration is a good thing, but you'd better be sitting at the typewriter when it hits" . . . Most professional writers work under a deadline, and you've got to sit down whether you have an idea or not. It all proceeds from a kind of discipline, and people who are waiting to be grabbed by the great idea, don't get much done.

Jerry: What do you think is the hardest thing about writing sitcom?

Eric: Well, the hardest thing about writing in general is making yourself do it.

Jerry: But what about the "business" part of the business?

Eric: The funny thing is that, now more than ever, a twenty-five-year-old starting out has an advantage over a fifty-year-old who's been doing it for years. There's never been more passion for youth . . . So the question that arises is: How does a fifty-year-old get back into the business? . . . And one of the ways is to go into business with a twenty-five-year-old. I was once teamed up with Max Shulman, who was my hero. I was twenty-six and doing *Welcome Back, Kotter,* and Max was sixty and unemployed. The man was probably the greatest living comedy writer—the Joe DiMaggio of comedy. Anyway, the point is, Max couldn't get a job unless they found a kid to work with him, and I was the kid . . . It hasn't changed as much as we think. What's changed is the fact that we're not kids anymore.

Jerry: Thanks, you've thoroughly depressed me. So, any secrets to selling a story and getting a script assignment?

Eric: Well, the freelance business is very difficult. Now, more than ever, shows are staff written. So, the way to get a job is to have a good writing sample. Even for experienced professionals. I've written hundreds of scripts, but still, from time to time, my agent will say: "Go write a spec."

Jerry: What kind of spec?

Eric: You pick out what is considered to be the best "writer's show," like a *Friends* or a *Frasier*. At any given point in time, there's this popular show that all the specs seem to be based on, and that's what you write.

Jerry: What do you think of the way stories are marketed—the pitch. Do you think there's a better way of doing this?

Eric: You're not making the rules. The hardest thing is to get a meeting. Most shows are not open to unknown writers . . . So, it's a by-the-numbers process, and you've got to have a good writing sample and then send it around to agents until you find somebody who will represent you and will get it to somebody who gets it to somebody. There's a whole continuum of ways that writers get their first jobs, and there's really no accounting for it.

Jerry: What do you think of the sitcoms on the air today?

Eric: I don't think there's been a quantum leap forward in the form. The biggest problem is a wholesale embrace of political correctness. Shows like *All in the Family* and *Maude* used to tackle subject matter that would be unthinkable today.

Jerry: Why unthinkable?

Eric: Unthinkable only in that the networks, the executives, and the studios are afraid of the heat they'll get.

Jerry: So it all has to do with America's overabundance of lawyers?

Eric: Quite possibly. We've taken several steps backwards. Today, people take umbrage at all sorts of things in a very organized fashion and, unfortunately, political correctness is the enemy of comedy. It's humorless. Tends to miss the point. I think that fair-minded people should be able to tell the difference between prejudice and comedy . . . Years ago, *Maude* did a two-part episode about abortion . . .

Jerry: . . . It's not even re-run today.

Eric: It's a hot-button topic, and there are strong feelings on both sides of the issue. There's Right to Life, a Woman's Right to Choose, and so on, and apparently the people who don't have a right to life are the comedy writers because there is no subject that can't be treated comically . . . To paraphrase Mark Twain: "There is nothing that can stand against a wave of laughter."

Jerry: I know you're probably asked this all the time, but what's your all-time favorite sitcom?

Eric: I have a couple that I love. Can I divide it up a bit?

Jerry: Divide away.

Eric: I would divide it by decade, by star, also in terms of where I was in life. As a kid, I idolized Jackie Gleason. *The Honeymooners* was so much a function of casting. It's unimaginable without Gleason and Carney, although in terms of writing and storytelling, it certainly wasn't the best . . . And the reason that *I Love Lucy* holds up so well is because no one has ever been better at broad physical comedy than she was. But, again, it wasn't a show that I would point to as an example of great writing.

Jerry: A tour de force.

Eric: Exactly. Now, to get into the world in which the writing and the acting mesh, I think you go to *The Dick Van Dyke Show*— a great marriage of performance and writing—stories pulled right from everyday life. The other one, just jumping back, was Phil Silvers . . .

Jerry: . . . *Sergeant Bilko.*

Eric: The *Bilkos* were well-written, well-acted . . . And *Dobie Gillis* . . . I loved *Dobie Gillis.*

Jerry: It had style.

Eric: And then, there's *Mary Tyler Moore,* and I was definitely on board with *Seinfeld.* Writers are told to make characters likable, and Larry David didn't do that. One of his guiding principles was that the *Seinfeld* characters never learned anything. They never got better. And no hugging. Nobody ever hugged.

Jerry: It went against all the rules . . .

Eric: . . . The rules are, there are no rules.

Jerry: Recall some of the performers you enjoyed working with.

Eric: The most professional cast I ever worked with was *The Golden Girls*. They committed to everything, and a cast like that makes a lot of stuff work, makes the writer look good. Writing for John Travolta on *Welcome Back, Kotter,* I'd go down to the rehearsal stage and, lo and behold, there'd be laughs where I didn't even anticipate laughs. A very gifted man.

Jerry: All the Sweathogs were a creative bunch.

Eric: Okay, make that four gifted men. Those kids jumped off the screen, and that's what you need. The best writing in the world won't keep your show on the air if your cast stinks.

Jerry: Another wise nugget. So, what kind of a project are you involved in now?

Eric: I'm in business with Edward James Olmos . . . We've developed a Latino situation comedy called *Three to Tango,* which somebody is definitely going to put on television.

Jerry: You sound pretty positive about this.

Eric: Well, I already wrote it once . . . We sold it to ABC last season.

Jerry: Sounds like Olmos has some clout.

Eric: It's like pitching with the president of Mexico.

Jerry: Just a couple more quick questions . . . If you weren't a comedy writer, what would you be?

Eric: Richer.

Jerry: And what advice would you give to a young sitcom writer starting out today?

Eric: Go to Harvard . . . work on the *Lampoon* . . . and write a good spec for *Friends.*

Jerry: *Friends,* you think?

Eric: Yeah, *Friends,* I think. Whatever the "writer's show" is at the moment.

Jerry: So, tell me, after all you've done in the business, do you have any regrets?

Eric: Oh, my God, more than I could name. I would do everything differently, okay?

Jerry: And where do you think you would've ended up?

Eric: I'd have eight of the top ten shows on television.
Jerry: EIGHT shows?
Eric: Well, I don't want to appear greedy.

I picked up the check and it was well worth it. It's not often you get so much comedy wisdom for the price of two corned beefs on rye.

THAT'S JUST ABOUT ALL, FOLKS!

Well, I didn't exactly make millions writing sitcom, but I did have a lot of fun, sucked in some major moola, and kept an awful lot of restaurants from going under.

Today, I watch the CREDITS of the current sitcoms and I seldom recognize a single writer's name. It's a GENERATIONAL industry, and (as Eric Cohen pointed out) a younger guard periodically takes over. I found that out a few years ago when I looked around and realized that most all of my contemporaries had drifted out of the business, and I had outlasted just about every writer in my TV comedy generation. Where the life expectancy for a writer in the field is five years at most, I lasted over four times as long. Why? I'm a masochist? No, c'mon, you know why. I had RESILIENCE! I had TENACITY!

STATE OF THE JOKE

What I am about to write here may no longer be true by the time you read it, but I don't think so because I truly feel that good sitcom writing is becoming extinct. But for a few exceptions, there are entirely too many funnyless shows on the air. Comedy is being punched down to the pits level, and viewers are having to settle for less, which is, if you ask me, a highly dangerous sociological trend, leading to a huge increase in gun sales.

The reason for this absurd situation is painfully apparent— the kids are running the shows. When I began my career in sitcom there was a MENTORING process supervised by older, more experienced comedy writers who taught young dudes and dudettes the finer points of crafting shows for laughs. I once had an office right next to the original writers of *I Love Lucy*. I learned a whole lot about writing comedy from quality professionals like these.

Today, the majority of sitcom writers are in their twenties and their mentors are a year or two older. Kids teaching kids. So much for mentoring. So much for laughs.

The kids also seem to be running the networks. Oh, sure, they may look like adults in their sharply tailored suits, but their minds seem to be cocooned in some kind of "arrested adolescence" where getting laid is more important than world peace. (No pun intended.)

The networks (including UPN, WB, and the rest) are failing to reflect our country as it is. They insist on serving a small, exclusively youngish segment of our population, claiming that this youthful demographic is the only segment of our population that buys products. Over forty, forget it. You're old, you're dead, you don't need toilet paper anymore.

I'm not done yet. I'm in an Andy Rooney mood, and here's another thing that bugs me. New sitcoms don't have a chance to succeed anymore. If you don't click in a couple of weeks, you're canceled. Classic shows like *All in the Family* and *The Dick Van Dyke Show* were not hits the first season, but the networks stuck with them and nurtured them into hits. *Cheers* had low ratings in season one, but the network showed a commitment to quality by renewing it. In its second season, the fine ensemble cast jelled and the audience was treated to some sensational TV. Had *Cheers* debuted today with low ratings, it would've been history in a week.

I certainly hope this kind of instant hit, cocaine mentality does not continue to rule the forces that present us with our TV comedy. Our nation's health depends on its citizens being exposed to good humor on a regular basis.

Luckily, life moves in cycles, as does sitcom, so I fully expect that shows of real substance and honest-to-goodness humor, supervised by seasoned professionals, will sprout from the comedy fields again. If this doesn't happen, sell your TV set and buy a Monopoly game.

THERE IS LIFE AFTER HOLLYWOOD

So, as I reflect on my sitcom experience, do I harbor any regrets? None at all. I'm indebted to a business that taught me (and paid me) so much—a business that provided me with memories I will always remember, and a few I've conveniently forgotten. I wear my experience with pride. I was one of the lucky ones who made it. And, today, I continue to make an excellent living writing humor from my home state of Wisconsin, but I never could have done it without my Hollywood experience.

I studied to be a high school teacher in college, and now here I am, years later, actually TEACHING! A great deal of my time is devoted to teaching HUMOR WRITING at various schools and universities. So, what can I teach you? Well, if you've actually read this entire book without skipping over parts, that pretty well takes care of it. Well, ALMOST takes care of it. Allow me to add this:

1. Pay attention in English class. I don't care if your teacher is a dip, it's a subject that will be very useful to you in your writing career.
2. Attend the occasional writing seminar and listen to what the pros have to say.
3. Become a student of sitcom—past and present. Study the shows. Analyze why the hits were hits.
4. Devote the same efforts to PERFORMANCE as you do to your writing. Public Speaking and Drama courses are essential to marketing yourself.
5. Visualize. SEE yourself as a successful TV comedy writer.

6. Reflect on the things we all experience in our daily lives in your own, unique way. There is no limit to what you can write about.

7. This final bit of advice comes from fellow writer E.B. White, who summed up the secret to any writer's success in two words: "Be Lucky."

BIG FINISH

Things have changed a lot since the days Ernie Kovacs and his cohorts invented comedy television. Today's environment is mired in a corporate sameness. It has achieved a bland, copycat mentality that is dangerous to creative people like us. It puts life in a shrinker, cuts off the channel to our imaginations, and encourages us to turn off our minds. Everything is prepackaged by cookie-cutterized accountants in corporate boardrooms. Ernie Kovacs never would have made it in television today because his unique brand of invention isn't easily monitored and controlled.

So, are you going to accept a situation like this? I certainly hope not! The promise of TV as an inventive tool is still there and it's up to you to furnish that invention. It's easy to copy, and that's the path many writers choose to take. DON'T be one of those writers! Dare to be an individual. Tenaciously pursue a new gonzoism and make those corporate creeps so much money they'll be forced to share some of it with you.

I hope this book will help you in your career quest, and I CHALLENGE you to go out and do what I did. Write everyday. Be productive. Avoid the pitfalls. Make me proud.

There's a guy in the wings waving a hook with my name on it, so I'm going to get off by reminding you that humor is a positive force that uplifts the human spirit. As a humorist, you have a responsibility to fashion a wake-up call for this and succeeding generations. And don't worry if you fail to get a big laugh—a simple smile is reward enough.

I've enjoyed our time together.

FADE OUT.

THE END

SITCOM AGENTS

The following is a list of agents who have a pretty good track record selling scripts and their writers to the witty world of sitcom.

I have tried to provide a list that is as up-to-date as possible. But, please be aware that we live in a time where agencies are constantly merging, moving, going out of business, or all three. It is not a complete agent list—for that, or any updates, contact the Writers' Guild Web site: *www.wga.com.*

Agency for the Performing Arts
9200 Sunset Blvd. #900
Los Angeles, CA 90069
(310) 888-4200

The Agency
1800 Avenue of the Stars #400
Los Angeles, CA 90067
(310) 551-3000

The Artists Agency
10000 Santa Monica Blvd. #305
Los Angeles, CA 90067
(310) 277-7779

Broder/Kurland/Webb/Uffner
9242 Beverly Blvd. #200
Beverly Hills, CA 90210
(310) 281-3400

The Coppage Company
3500 West Olive #1420
Burbank, CA 91505
(818) 953-4163

Creative Artists Agency (CAA)
9830 Wilshire Blvd.
Beverly Hills, CA 90212
(323) 288-4545

Douroux & Co.
445 South Beverly Drive #310
Beverly Hills, CA 90212
(310) 552-0900

Dytman & Associates
9200 Sunset Blvd. #809
Los Angeles, CA 90069
(310) 274-8844

The Endeavor Agency
9701 Wilshire Blvd., 10th Floor
Beverly Hills, CA 90212
(310) 248-2000

The Gersh Agency, Inc.
232 North Canon Drive #201
Beverly Hills, CA 90210
(310) 274-6611

Larry Grossman & Associates
211 South Beverly Drive #206
Beverly Hills, CA 90212
(310) 550-8127

Innovative Artists
1999 Avenue of the Stars #2850
Los Angeles, CA 90067
(310) 553-5200

International Creative Management (ICM)
8942 Wilshire Blvd.
Beverly Hills, CA 90211
(310) 550-4000

The Kaplan/Stahler/Gumer Agency
8383 Wilshire Blvd. #923
Beverly Hills, CA 90211
(323) 653-4483

The Candace Lake Agency
9200 Sunset Blvd. #820
Los Angeles, CA 90069
(310) 247-2115

Major Clients Agency
345 North Maple Drive #395
Beverly Hills, CA 90210
(310) 205-5000

Metropolitan Talent Agency
4526 Wilshire Blvd.
Los Angeles, CA 90010
(323) 857-4500

The William Morris Agency
151 El Camino Drive
Beverly Hills, CA 90212
(310) 274-7451

Paradigm
10100 Santa Monica Blvd. #2500
Los Angeles, CA 90067
(310) 277-4400

The Barry Perelman Agency
9200 Sunset Blvd. #1201
Los Angeles, CA 90069
(310) 274-5999

Preferred Artists
16633 Ventura Blvd. #1421
Encino, CA 91436
(818) 990-0305

The Jim Preminger Agency
1650 Westwood Blvd. #201
Los Angeles, CA 90024
(310) 475-9491

The Rothman Agency
9465 Wilshire Blvd. #840
Beverly Hills, CA 90212
(310) 247-9898

The Irv Schechter Company
9300 Wilshire Blvd., Suite 400
Beverly Hills, CA 90212
(310) 278-8070

Shapiro/Lichtman/Stein
8827 Beverly Blvd.
Los Angeles, CA 90048
(310) 859-8877

United Talent Agency
9560 Wilshire Blvd., 5th Floor
Beverly Hills, CA 90212
(310) 273-6700

Vision Art Management
9200 Sunset Blvd., Penthouse #1
Los Angeles, CA 90069
(310) 888-3288

Writers & Artists Agency
924 Westwood Blvd. #900
Los Angeles, CA 90024
(310) 824-6300

WRITERS' GUILD OF AMERICA QUALIFICATIONS FOR MEMBERSHIP

The requirements for admission into the Writers' Guild of America west are detailed in a lengthy four-page, single-spaced, legal document that I would like to simplify in plain English. Sorry to disappoint all you lawyers out there. (If you wish to see the legal document in its entirety, it can be found at: *www.wga.org.*)

Qualification for union membership is based upon a UNIT system earned for various stages and types of scripting, or weeks employed as a staff writer. Here are the facts as applied to writers in the thirty-minute sitcom field:

- A total of twenty-four UNITS are required for membership.
- The company you work for must be a signatory to the WGA Collective Bargaining Agreement.
- If you are credited for only STORY in a thirty-minute teleplay, you are given four UNITS.

- If you are given credit for only TELEPLAY in a thirty-minute script, you get eight UNITS.
- When you receive credit for both STORY & TELEPLAY, you are credited with twelve UNITS.
- You are assigned two UNITS for every week you serve as staff writer on a show. (Twelve weeks and you're in.)
- The twenty-four UNITS are awarded in increments, and must be accumulated within the three years preceding your application for membership.
- If you write a teleplay in COLLABORATION with another writer, both writers are treated as individuals in being credited for units. (So, in this case, two heads ARE better.)
- If you're a major dreamer and your theatrical motion picture screenplay is produced (ninety minutes or longer), you get all twenty-four UNITS in one swoop—which is why it so hard to attain this rarified brand of swooping.

Once you have accumulated the necessary twenty-four UNITS for membership, a cashier's check or money order, payable to the Writers' Guild of America west, Inc. in the amount of $2,500, is due. A mere drop in the bucket now that you're rolling in the big dough.

It is advised that writers residing West of the Mississippi River apply for membership in the WGA west. Writers residing East of the Mississippi River should contact the Writers' Guild of America East, 555 West 57th St., New York, NY 10019, (212) 767-7800.

Now, if you're a writer who lives on a raft exactly in middle of the Mississippi, this may cause some confusion, but—as I've said earlier—the strength of TV comedy lies out West, so West is where you should be headed.

WRITERS' GUILD OF AMERICA

Writers' Guild of America west
7000 W. Third Street
Los Angeles, CA 90048
Web site: *www.wga.org*
Main number: (323) 951-4000

DEPARTMENTS:
Agency: (323) 782-4502
Claims: (323) 782-4663
Contracts: (323) 782-4501
Credits: (323) 782-4528
Dues: (323) 782-4531
Employment Access: (323) 782-4548
Legal Services: (323) 782-4521
Library: (323) 782-4544
Member Services: (323) 782-4747
Membership: (323) 782-4532
Publications: (323) 782-4542
Registration: (323) 782-4500
Residuals: (323) 782-4700

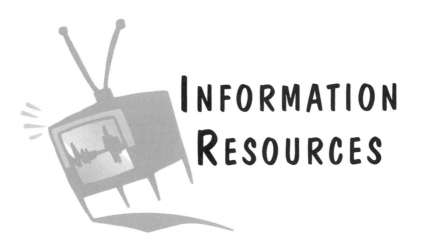

INFORMATION RESOURCES

TRADE PUBLICATIONS

DAILY VARIETY
5700 Wilshire Blvd. #120
Los Angeles, CA 90036
(323) 857-6600
(323) 857-0494 (FAX)
Features all the daily news of the show biz trade.
Subscription: $219.00 per year. California residents add 8¼ percent sales tax.

HOLLYWOOD REPORTER
5055 Wilshire Blvd., 5th Floor
Los Angeles, CA 90036
(323) 525-2150
(323) 525-2387 (FAX)
Web site: *subscriptions@hollywoodreporter.com*
Trade daily covering all the latest in the entertainment industry.
Subscription: $219.00 per year. California residents add 8¼ percent sales tax.

HOLLYWOOD SCRIPTWRITER
P.O. Box 10277
Burbank, CA 91510
(818) 845-5525
(818) 709-7540 (FAX)
e-mail: *lgrantt@earthlink.net*
Web site: *www.hollywoodscriptwriter.com*
Twelve-page monthly newsletter of interviews plus information on agents, markets, workshops, you name it.
Subscription: $35.00 per year

WRITTEN BY
The Journal of the Writers' Guild
7000 West Third St.
Los Angeles, CA 90048-9968
(323) 782-4522
(323) 782-4802 (FAX)
Web site: *writtenby@wga.org*
The official (monthly) publication of the Writers' Guild of America. Features articles by the pros and a TV Marketing List that gives you the lowdown on who's producing what show and where you can track them down. You do not have to be a member to subscribe.
Subscription: $40.00 per year/single issues $5.00/student rate with ID

ONLINE: HOLLYWOOD CREATIVE DIRECTORY
Web site: *www.hcdonline.com*
Publishes six directories listing production companies, TV and film executives, agents and managers—with titles, addresses, phone/fax numbers, and samples of their credits. Postings such as: Hollywood Job Board and Hollywood Classifieds (which includes workshops, seminars, and professional services).
Subscription: $129.95 per year plus $4 shipping per book.

PROFESSIONAL ORGANIZATONS

ACADEMY OF TELEVISION ARTS & SCIENCES
5220 Lankershim Blvd.
North Hollywood, CA 91601
(818) 754-2800
Web site: *www.emmy.org*
Dedicated to the promotion and preservation of the television arts.

AMERICAN FILM INSTITUTE
2021 N. Western Ave.
Los Angeles, CA 90027
(323) 856-7600
Web site: *www.afionline.org*
Not only focused on film, but also dedicated to the advancement of
the television arts. Lots of industry workshops.

NATIONAL WRITERS' CLUB
3140 South Peoria St. #295
Aurora, CO 80014
(303) 841-0246
e-mail: *sandywrter@aol.com*
Web site: *www.nationalwriters.com*
Information on all kinds of writing events. Sponsors a writing confer-
ence the second weekend in June.

WOMEN IN FILM
6464 Sunset Blvd. #1080
Los Angeles, CA 90028
(323) 463-6040
(323) 463-0963 (FAX)
Web site: *www.wif.org*
Geared toward women in film, TV, and other media. Sponsors seminars; publishes a monthly newsletter.

TELEVISION SCRIPTS

SCRIPT CITY
8033 Sunset Blvd. #1500
Hollywood, CA 90046
1-800-676-2522
FREE complimentary catalogue available.

SAMUEL FRENCH THEATRE & FILM BOOKSHOP
7623 Sunset Blvd.
Los Angeles, CA 90046
(323) 876-0570

LARRY EDMUNDS CINEMA & THEATRE BOOK SHOP
6644 Hollywood Blvd.
Hollywood, CA 90028
(323) 463-3273

EDUCATIONAL OPPORTUNITIES

Writing seminars and workshops abound in this great land of ours, and they are far too numerous to mention here. To find out about what's going on in your neck of the woods, call the communications department of your nearby college or university.

As for specific schools for TV Comedy Writing, I can't think of any. The best way to learn comedy writing is by reading this book, getting all of your friends to buy this book, and then taking the time to just sit down and write. If you possess the knack for seeing life as the nuthouse it is, you're well on your way.

Going to the occasional seminar or workshop is cool because you'll likely pick up bits of helpful wisdom from a professional. BUT, writers teach themselves to write by writing, not attending classes. Many of our funniest writers never went to college, some never went to school at all, and those who went to Harvard will never be shy about telling you so.

Writing can be a lonely profession, and if you need to social-ize with folks in a classroom in order to feel motivated, forget it. If you can't find the motivation within yourself, get a partner. If you can't find a partner, reread this book.

INDEX

payment for, 161
as rough draft, 890
story development in, 71–72
format. *see* script format
Foxx, Red
Sanford & Sons, 160
Frasier, 19, 21, 27–28, 29, 43, 107, 153, 183
Friends, 183, 185

Gleason, Jackie, 115
The Honeymooners, 184
The Gersh Agency, 193
The Golden Girls, 177, 185

Happy Days, 15, 132, 148, 173
Harper Valley PTA
"The Show Must Go On," 116–121
Head of the Class, 15
"I Am The King," 32–38, 42, 44,
45–47, 70
scene notes on, 48–58
"Past Imperfect," 102–103
"We Love You, Mrs. Russell," 109–110
Helton, Percy, 104
Hemingway, Ernest, 46
Hessman, Howard, 20
Hollywood, 173–174
Hollywood Reporter, 201
Hollywood Scriptwriter, 202
Home Improvement, 76
The Honeymooners, 184
Howdy Doody, 15
humor, 9–11. *see also* comedy; jokes
and action, 115
certain words of, 85–86
and character, 79
key to, 95
out of character, 76
uplifting nature of, 190
humor exercises
bizarre questions/answers, 11
cartoons, 12
embellishment, 11, 19–20
exaggeration, 11
jokes, 12
make fun at yourself, 12
hunch, 92

I Love Lucy, 175, 184, 188
Innovative Artists, 193
inspiration, 182
International Creative Management
(ICM), 126, 193
Irving, John, 25

Jewishness, 180
jokes, 12, 71, 85, 91, 93
crude, 87
definition of, 99
as double entendre, 98–99
exaggeration in, 94–95
familiarity and, 96
as malaprop, 98
non-sequitor, 98
punchline of, 94
and puns, 99–100
as reversal of thought process, 96–97
rhythm of, 103
set-up of, 94
surprise factor in, 95, 180
techniques of, 96–100
three per page rule for, 100–102
unpredictable nature of, 94
utilize imagery in, 98
as verbal deception, 93
word placement in, 103–104
wordplay use in, 97–98, 99
The Jonathan Winters Show, 5
Just Shoot Me, 41

Kalmar, Bert
Duck Soup, 99
Kaplan, Gabe, 155–156, 179
The Kaplan/Stahler/Gumer Agency, 193
Kaufman, George S.
Animal Crackers, 99
Keaton, Buster, 115
Komack, James, 100, 146
Kovacs, Ernie, 4, 190

The Candance **L**ake Agency, 193
Langford, Frances, 1
Larry Edmunds Cinema & Theatre Book
Shop, 204
Larry Grossman & Associates, 193
laughtracks, 175
Laverne & Shirley, 177
Lawrence, Martin
Martin, 116
lawyer, 158
Lewis, Jerry, 16
Lithgow, John, 19
Lloyd, Harold, 115
log line, 168
Los Angeles, 173–174
Love, American Style, 6, 30, 127, 132, 148
luck, 190

major ("A") story, 29–30, 48, 49
Major Clients Agency, 193

BOOKS FROM ALLWORTH PRESS

Selling Scripts to Hollywood by Katherine Atwell Herbert (softcover, 6 × 9, 176 pages, $12.95)

The Screenwriter's Legal Guide, Second Edition by Stephen F. Breimer (softcover, 6 × 9, 320 pages, $19.95)

The Writer's Legal Guide, Second Edition by Tad Crawford and Tony Lyons (hardcover, 6 × 9, 320 pages, $19.95)

Writing Scripts Hollywood Will Love: An Insider's Guide to Film and Television Scripts that Sell by Katherine Atwell Herbert (softcover, 6 × 9, 160 pages, $12.95)

The Copyright Guide: A Friendly Guide for Protecting and Profiting from Copyrights by Lee Wilson (softcover, 6 × 9, 192 pages, $18.95)

Marketing Strategies for Writers by Michael Sedge (softcover, 6 × 9, 224 pages, $16.95)

Writing.com: Creative Internet Strategies to Advance Your Writing Career by Moira Anderson Allen (softcover, 6 × 9, 256 pages, $16.95)

How to Write Books That Sell, Second Edition by L. Perry Wilbur and Jon Samsel (hardcover, 6 × 9, 224 pages, $19.95)

How to Write Articles That Sell, Second Edition by L. Perry Wilbur and Jon Samsel (hardcover, 6 × 9, 224 pages, $19.95)

The Complete Guide to Book Marketing by David Cole (softcover, 6 × 9, 288 pages, $19.95)

The Complete Guide to Book Publicity by Jodee Blanco (softcover, 6 × 9, 288 pages, $19.95)

Business and Legal Forms for Authors and Self-Publishers, Revised Edition by Tad Crawford (softcover, includes CD-ROM, $8\frac{1}{2}$ × 11, 192 pages, $22.95)

Mastering the Business of Writing: A Leading Literary Agent Reveals the Secrets of Success by Richard Curtis (softcover, 6 × 9, 272 pages, $18.95)

The Writer's Resource Handbook by Daniel Grant (softcover, 6 × 9, 272 pages, $19.95)

Please write to request our free catalog. To order by credit card, call 1-800-491-2808 or send a check or money order to Allworth Press, 10 East 23rd Street, Suite 210, New York, NY 10010. Include $5 for shipping and handling for the first book ordered and $1 for each additional book. Ten dollars plus $1 for each additional book if ordering from Canada. New York State residents must add sales tax.

To see our complete catalog on the World Wide Web, or to order online, you can find us at *www.allworth.com*.